ANNE WILLAN'S
LOOK&COOK

Chocolate Desserts

ANNE WILLAN'S
LOOK&COOK
Chocolate Desserts

DORLING KINDERSLEY
LONDON • NEW YORK • STUTTGART

A DORLING KINDERSLEY BOOK

Created and Produced by
CARROLL & BROWN LTD
5 Lonsdale Road
London NW6 6RA

Editorial Director Jeni Wright
Editors Norma MacMillan
Stella Vayne
Art Editor Mary Staples
Designers Lyndel Donaldson
Wendy Rogers
Lucy de Rosa
Lisa Webb

First published in Great Britain in 1992
by Dorling Kindersley Limited
9 Henrietta Street, London WC2E 8PS

A CIP catalogue record for this book is available
from the British Library
ISBN 0-86318-863-X

Reproduced by Colourscan, Singapore
Printed and bound in Italy by A. Mondadori, Verona

CONTENTS

CHOCOLATE

THE LOOK & COOK APPROACH

W elcome to **Chocolate Desserts,** and the *Look & Cook* series. These volumes are designed to be the simplest, most informative cookbooks you'll ever own. They are the closest I can come to sharing my personal techniques for cooking my favourite recipes without actually being with you in the kitchen.

EQUIPMENT

Equipment and ingredients often determine whether or not you can cook a particular dish, so *Look & Cook* illustrates everything you need at the beginning of each recipe. You'll see at a glance how long a recipe takes to cook, how many servings it makes, what the finished dish looks like, and how much preparation can be done ahead. When you start to cook, you'll find the preparation and cooking are organised into easy-to-follow steps. Each stage is colour-coded and everything is shown in photographs with brief text to go with each step. You will never be in doubt as to what it is you are doing, why you are doing it, or how it should look.

INGREDIENTS

🍽 SERVES 8 🥣 WORK TIME 25-30 MINUTES 🍲 BAKING TIME 25-30 MINUTES

I've also included helpful hints and ideas under 'Anne Says'. These may list an alternative ingredient or piece of equipment, explain a certain method, or advise on mastering a particular technique. Similarly, if there is a crucial stage in a recipe when things can go wrong, I've included some warnings called 'Take Care'.

Many of the photographs are annotated to pinpoint why certain pieces of equipment work best, or how the food should look at that stage of cooking. Because presentation is so important, a picture of the finished dish and serving suggestions are at the end of each recipe. Many simple ideas for decoration are included, but a few, such as piped fans, will challenge the accomplished cook.

Thanks to all this information, you can't go wrong. I'll be with you every step of the way. So please, come with me into the kitchen to look, cook and create some stunning **Chocolate Desserts.**

Anne Willan

WHY CHOCOLATE?

*Whose eyes do not light up at the sight of a luscious chocolate dessert?
You may debate the merits of white versus dark chocolate, or which brand is best,
and whether the high cocoa butter content of covering chocolate (couverture) makes
it preferable to other types, but there is no disagreement that chocolate is everyone's
favourite. Indeed, it is so versatile that you might even be tempted to limit your
dessert repertoire to this fabulous flavour. Your guests will surely applaud!*

RECIPE CHOICE

No matter what its origin, a chocolate dessert needs no passport. European chocolate tortes and mousses are as eagerly received as American cakes and ice creams. Some cooks find chocolate temperamental, but once you understand how it works, you will have no trouble. In this volume, I'll be showing you how to make perfect cake mixtures, fillings, icings and garnishes. Chocolate decorations, which offer so much variety, are featured in many recipes. There is something for everyone – from light, airy soufflés and chocolate sorbet to sumptuously rich cakes and crispy chocolate crème brûlée.

CHOCOLATE CAKES

For everyday occasions plain chocolate cakes are ideal. *Chocolate Orange Pound Cake*: flavoured with homemade candied orange peel and topped with a light orange icing. *Chocolate Orange Marble Pound Cake*: chocolate orange and plain orange mixtures are swirled to create a marbled effect. *Speckled Chocolate Cake*: curls of dark chocolate hide a moist cake speckled with nuggets of chopped chocolate. *Chocolate Butterfly Cakes*: a children's treat; tops of individual chocolate cakes settle on filling to resemble butterfly wings.

Well-beloved European favourites are among my classic choices. *Chocolate Walnut Torte*: rich and laden with ground nuts and dark chocolate, topped with Chantilly cream. *Chocolate Almond Torte:* another flourless cake, this dense almond torte is topped with a lattice of sprinkled icing sugar and cocoa. *Sachertorte:* the world-famous rich chocolate cake hailing from Austria.

Chocolate Raspberry Torte: served with fresh raspberries, this lavish version of Sachertorte has a glaze of raspberry jam under silky icing. *Black Forest Cake*: from the Black Forest of Germany comes this cake flavoured with kirsch, layered with Chantilly cream and black cherries. *Black Forest Strip Cake*: when shaped in a rectangle, Black Forest cake is easy to slice. *Chocolate Praline Cake:* chocolate layer cake with rum syrup and crunchy caramel-almond praline.

Roulades or roll cakes feature a variety of fillings. *Chocolate Chestnut Roll*: a winter filling of chestnut, whipped cream and dark rum. *Chocolate Strawberry Cream Cake*: a must with fresh, sweet summer strawberries. *Chocolate Nut Cream Cake with Caramel Sauce*: hazelnuts and caramel pair deliciously in another version of a chocolate roll.

Now for the ultimate chocolate cakes. *Chocolate Orange Truffle Cake*: rich, thick ganache flavoured with Grand Marnier crowns a light sponge cake. *Chocolate Coffee Truffle Cake*: chocolate addicts beware! *Chequerboard Cake with Chocolate Ganache*: a surprise awaits beneath the rich ganache frosting of this eye-catching chocolate and vanilla chequerboard cake. *Apricot Chequerboard Cake*: apricots make a tart-sweet, golden sauce, providing a delicious contrast with this chequerboard cake.

For a superlative finish to any meal, choose from my trio of chocolate cheesecakes. *Chocolate Marble Cheesecake*: swirls of chocolate and plain cheesecake fillings in a delectable dessert. *All-Chocolate Cheesecake*: for chocolate purists. *White Chocolate Cheesecake*: a cream-coloured mixture with white chocolate fills this cheesecake.

CHOCOLATE DESSERTS

Chocolate-flavoured custards and creams are great for special occasions. *Chocolate Crème Brûlée*: the classic crème brûlée with a chocolate accent. *Chocolate Crème Brûlée with Raspberries:* fresh raspberries are concealed with the chocolate cream under the topping of caramelised sugar. *Chocolate Mousse with Hazelnuts and Whisky:* who can say 'no' to chocolate mousse with the nutty bite of hazelnuts, and whisky? *Double-Chocolate Mousse*: chunks of white chocolate contrast with smooth dark chocolate mousse.

Mousse and more make three great desserts. *Black and White Chocolate Mousse Towers*: discs of dark chocolate layered with white chocolate mousse and blueberries, form individual towers in pools of raspberry coulis. *Dark Chocolate Whisky Mousse Towers*: the filling of dark chocolate mousse laced with whisky is spiked with plump blueberries. *Marbled Black and White Chocolate Mousse Towers:* here dark chocolate squares are feathered with white chocolate and layered with white chocolate mousse and delicious fresh raspberries.

Hot desserts are also impressive. *Chocolate Soufflé*: light as air and deliciously rich. *Individual Chocolate Soufflés*: single serving portions of an all-time favourite. *Amaretto Chocolate Soufflé*: almond biscuits soaked in almond liqueur are hidden in the centre of this soufflé. *Steamed Mexican Chocolate Pudding with Apricot Sauce*: this classic steamed pudding is spiced with cinnamon and cloves and served with an apricot sauce. *Steamed Mexican Chocolate Pudding with Chocolate Sauce*: the same spicy pudding with a hot, dark chocolate sauce.

Chocolate and pastry combined create elegant desserts. *Chocolate and Pear Tartlets*: a great fruit and chocolate match, with a topping of thinly sliced fresh pear.

Chocolate and Apple Tartlets: chunks of apple, sautéed with sugar and cinnamon, top the chocolate in these little tarts. *Profiteroles with Chocolate Ice Cream:* puffs of choux pastry are filled with rich chocolate ice cream, topped with a contrasting hot chocolate sauce. *Chocolate Ice Cream Swans*: choux pastry baked in elegant swan shapes, filled with ice cream and floating on a lake of rich chocolate sauce. *Choux Chantilly Ring*: chocolate sauce accompanies a ring of choux pastry filled with airy Chantilly cream.

Incredibly dark and delicious are the following. *Chocolate Charlotte*: half fudge, half cake, this intense chocolate mould swathed in Chantilly cream is the perfect winter treat. *Small Chocolate Charlottes*: a charlotte per person, for devout chocolate lovers.

ICED CHOCOLATE DESSERTS

Enjoy the ice creams and sorbets on their own or use to top or fill other treats. *Chocolate Ice Cream*: rich and delicious, loved by one and all. *Chocolate Indulgence Ice Cream*: an indulgence indeed! *Chocolate Praline Ice Cream*: the nutty crunch of praline with the sweet smoothness of chocolate ice cream. *Chocolate Mocha Sorbet*: coffee adds delicious intensity to chocolate sorbet. *Chocolate Sorbet*: the impact of this ultra-simple sorbet, made with bittersweet chocolate, is a surprise.

Some eye-catching desserts to end. *Chocolate and Apricot Bombe*: elegant moulded dessert of chocolate ice cream, filled with a creamy apricot mixture and served with chocolate fudge sauce. *Bombe Royale*: what could be better than Swiss roll, chocolate ice cream and the tang of apricot brandy! *Chef Ferré's Frozen Tri-Chocolate Terrine*: from a top Paris pastry chef comes this iced terrine with layers of white, milk and dark chocolate, served on a pool of mint custard sauce. *Tri-Chocolate Terrine on Strawberry Coulis*: this time the creamy layered dessert is offset by fresh strawberry coulis.

EQUIPMENT

I've deliberately chosen these recipes to require little in the way of special equipment. However, the cakes do need specific tins of certain shapes and sizes. It is not advisable to change the sizes of the cake tins because the mixture will not bake correctly. The cheesecake uses a springform tin, while the chocolate terrines and bombes call for special moulds. Many of the desserts can be made in individual versions so you will find mousse pots and both small and large ramekins or soufflé dishes useful, but ovenproof *demitasse* cups can be substituted. A piping bag and a selection of different nozzles are important for piping some of the fillings and decorations. An ice-cream maker is necessary for the ice creams and sorbet.

INGREDIENTS

Chocolate takes kindly to a wide variety of other ingredients. Toasted and ground nuts add texture and flavour to chocolate cakes and fillings.

Cream adds lightness and a contrast of colour, while coffee transforms chocolate into mocha.

Juicy berries – raspberries, strawberries, blueberries and their cousins – are classic accompaniments, often as a coulis or sauce. Fresh fruits – notably oranges, apricots, cherries, pears and apples – are often paired with chocolate or used in a delicious jam glaze.

Another way to balance the richness of chocolate is by adding rum, whisky or brandy, or liqueurs such as Grand Marnier or kirsch.

TECHNIQUES

Working with chocolate needs care, but once you have mastered a handful of techniques your repertoire of chocolate desserts will expand quickly.

The building blocks for many of my recipes are important basics such as chopping, grating and melting chocolate. Melted chocolate is also the foundation for a wide variety of decorative techniques – for piping shapes, such as fans, and for spreading to make leaves. 'How-To' boxes will help you master them. Melted chocolate can be spread flat to make a ribbon for wrapping round a cake, or to cut into an assortment of shapes – squares, triangles and discs.

To improve the gloss of many of these decorations, professionals often temper chocolate, and on page 123 I show you an easy and reliable method.

Because so many of the chocolate recipes call for garnishes and because chocolate decorations are so popular with other types of desserts, there is further information on making chocolate decorations, with photographs of the finished results, in Chocolate Know-How.

As with the other volumes in this series, I have also included techniques for the other ingredients that are used in these chocolate recipes. For instance, you will find out how to make Chantilly cream, caramel cream sauce, berry coulis and jam glaze; how to toast and skin nuts; how to make candied orange peel, and make and crush praline; how to cut and fold mixtures together; how to separate eggs and whisk egg whites. There are instructions for making a paper piping cone, as well as for filling a piping bag, for lining a round cake tin, and for lining and flouring a loaf tin.

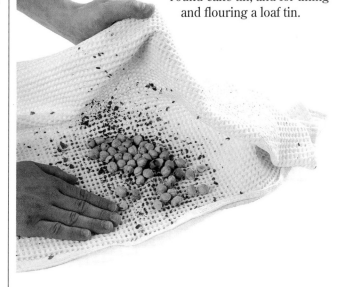

CHOCOLATE WALNUT TORTE

EQUIPMENT

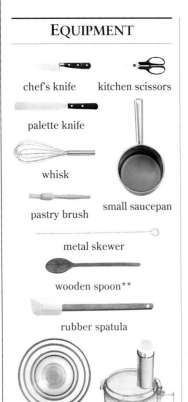

chef's knife   kitchen scissors

palette knife

whisk

pastry brush   small saucepan

metal skewer

wooden spoon**

rubber spatula

bowls

food processor***

chopping board   20-25 rose leaves

23-cm (9-inch) springform tin   plate

baking parchment

** electric mixer can also be used
*** blender can also be used

A torte in the true tradition of flourless cakes, this Chocolate Walnut Torte is based on ground walnuts and chocolate, lightened with meringue. The mixture is baked slowly in a low oven so the edges of the cake do not dry and the end result is beautifully moist. The Chantilly cream and piped chocolate add a luxurious finishing touch.

GETTING AHEAD

The torte can be prepared and baked up to 1 week ahead and kept in an airtight container. Make the Chantilly cream and add the chocolate topping not more than 2 hours before serving.

plus cooling and chilling time

metric	SHOPPING LIST	imperial
	butter and flour for tin	
375 g	plain chocolate	12 oz
250 g	walnut pieces	8 oz
4	eggs	4
125 g	unsalted butter	4 oz
200 g	caster sugar	6 ½ oz
For the Chantilly cream		
250 ml	double cream	8 fl oz
15 ml	caster sugar	1 tbsp
2.5 ml	vanilla essence	½ tsp

INGREDIENTS

plain chocolate   walnut pieces

eggs   double cream

unsalted butter   vanilla essence

sugar

ANNE SAYS
'Unsalted butter is important in pastries and cake fillings because its flavour is sweet and rich. Salted butter gives a sharper flavour.'

ORDER OF WORK

1 MAKE THE TORTE MIXTURE

2 BAKE THE TORTE AND MAKE THE CHOCOLATE LEAVES

3 FINISH THE TORTE

HOW TO LINE A ROUND CAKE TIN

Lining a cake tin with baking parchment ensures that the cake will not stick. If the mixture is rich, the tin should also be floured so that any excess butter is absorbed.

1 Melt 30-45 ml (2-3 tbsp) butter and brush inside the tin with an even coating, making sure the bottom and top edges are covered.

2 Fold a square of baking parchment in quarters, then in triangular eighths. Hold the point of the paper triangle over the centre of the tin and cut the paper even with the inside edge. Unfold the paper and press it on to the bottom of the tin. Butter the paper.

3 If directed in the recipe, flour the tin: sprinkle in 30-45 ml (2-3 tbsp) flour, then turn and shake the tin so that the flour evenly coats the bottom and side. Tap the tin to remove all excess flour.

1 MAKE THE TORTE MIXTURE

1 Heat the oven to 150°C (300°F, Gas 2). Butter, line and flour the tin (see box, left). Chop 110 g (3 ½ oz) of the chocolate and grind with half of the walnuts in the food processor or blender. Repeat with another 110 g (3 ½ oz) chocolate and the remaining nuts. (If using a blender, grind the chocolate and nuts in 4 batches.)

ANNE SAYS
'*For a finer texture, grind the nuts in a rotary hand grater. Then mix the nuts with the chocolate after it has been chopped.*'

3 Add the egg yolks one by one, beating thoroughly after each addition.

2 Separate the eggs (see box, page 12). With the wooden spoon, cream the butter. Add three-quarters of the sugar and beat until light and fluffy, 2-3 minutes.

Add ground chocolate and walnut mixture to creamed mixture all at once

4 Stir the ground chocolate and walnut mixture into the mixture using the rubber spatula.

5 Whisk the egg whites until stiff. Sprinkle in the remaining sugar and continue whisking until glossy.

6 Add the meringue to the chocolate mixture and fold them together using the rubber spatula.

2 BAKE THE TORTE AND MAKE THE CHOCOLATE LEAVES

1 Transfer the torte mixture to the prepared tin and smooth the top with the spatula.

2 Bake until the skewer inserted in the centre of the torte comes out clean, 60-70 minutes.

3 Allow the torte to cool completely in the tin. When completely cold, release the hinge on the side of the cake tin and lift it gently away from the cake.

ANNE SAYS
'The torte is so delicate, it is best served still on the base of the cake tin.'

4 Make the chocolate leaves: melt 125 g (4 oz) of the remaining chocolate. Using the pastry brush, spread chocolate on the shiny side of the rose leaves in a thin, even layer, leaving a little of the stems exposed. Place the leaves on a plate and allow to cool, then refrigerate until set. With the tips of your fingers, peel the leaves away from the chocolate.

HOW TO SEPARATE EGGS

Eggs are easy to separate by using the shell. However, if an egg is contaminated with salmonella, bacteria can cling to the shell and spread. Alternative methods are filtering the white through your fingers or using an egg separator.

1 **To separate an egg with the shell:** crack the egg at its broadest point by tapping it against a bowl. With 2 thumbs, break it open, letting some white slip over the edge of the shell into the bowl.

2 Tip yolk from one half of the shell to the other, detaching the remaining white from the yolk. If some yolk slips into the white, remove it with the shell. To remove white threads, pinch them against side of shell with your fingertips.

To separate an egg with your fingers: crack the egg into a bowl. Hold your cupped fingers over another bowl and let the white fall through them, leaving the yolk.

3 FINISH THE TORTE

1 Make the Chantilly cream: whip the cream in a bowl set in a larger bowl of iced water until soft peaks form. Add the sugar and vanilla and whip until soft peaks form again.

2 With the palette knife, spread the cream evenly over the top and side of the cake. Place the cake on a serving plate and chill about 1 hour.

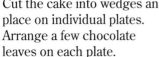
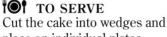

3 For the topping, chop the remaining 30 g (1 oz) chocolate and melt it in a bowl placed in a saucepan of hot water. Make a paper piping cone and fill with the chocolate. Pipe the chocolate lightly over the cake in a linear design. Clean the plate if necessary, and arrange the chocolate leaves around the edge.

ANNE SAYS
'Rather than piping on the chocolate, you can drizzle it over the cake with a teaspoon.'

†❂† TO SERVE
Cut the cake into wedges and place on individual plates. Arrange a few chocolate leaves on each plate.

Piped chocolate topping is simple to do but looks very special

Chocolate leaves are a beautiful decoration for any cake or dessert

VARIATION
CHOCOLATE ALMOND TORTE
Almonds add crunch to this variation of Chocolate Walnut Torte.

1 Replace the walnuts with the same quantity of whole blanched almonds. Toast the almonds before grinding, and make the cake as directed.
2 Omit the Chantilly cream and chocolate topping and decorate the cake as follows: cut four to five 2-cm (³/₄-inch) wide strips of thin card and lay them on top of the cake. Sprinkle with icing sugar. Carefully lift off the strips and discard the excess sugar.

3 Lay the strips back on the cake to make a diagonal lattice on the sugar bands. Sift cocoa powder generously over the top, and carefully lift off the card strips, discarding the excess cocoa powder.

CHOCOLATE ORANGE POUND CAKE

🍽 SERVES 6-8 🥄 WORK TIME ABOUT 2 HOURS* 🍲 BAKING TIME 50-60 MINUTES

EQUIPMENT

saucepans

sieve

kitchen scissors

loaf tin

ovenproof plate

chef's knife

small knife

pastry brush

slotted spoon

electric mixer

bowls

wire rack

chopping board

baking tray

squeezer

wooden spoon

baking parchment

rubber spatula

metal skewer

INGREDIENTS

plain flour

oranges

icing sugar

eggs

unsalted butter

baking powder

caster sugar

cocoa powder

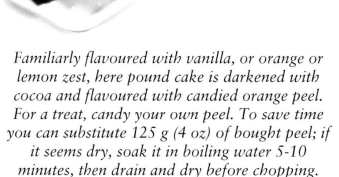

Familiarly flavoured with vanilla, or orange or lemon zest, here pound cake is darkened with cocoa and flavoured with candied orange peel. For a treat, candy your own peel. To save time you can substitute 125 g (4 oz) of bought peel; if it seems dry, soak it in boiling water 5-10 minutes, then drain and dry before chopping.

GETTING AHEAD

The cake can be stored up to 1 week in an airtight container.

* plus about 1 day soaking and drying for orange peel

metric	SHOPPING LIST	imperial
For the chocolate pound cake		
2	medium oranges	2
400 g	caster sugar	13 oz
250 ml	water	8 fl oz
	butter and flour for tin	
125 g	plain flour	4 oz
45 ml	cocoa powder	3 tbsp
5 ml	baking powder	1 tsp
	salt	
175 g	unsalted butter	6 oz
3	eggs	3
For the orange icing		
60 g	icing sugar	2 oz
10-15 ml	orange juice (reserved from orange for peel)	2-3 tsp

ORDER OF WORK

1 MAKE THE CHOCOLATE POUND CAKE

2 MAKE THE ORANGE ICING

3 ICE AND DECORATE THE CAKE

1 MAKE THE CHOCOLATE POUND CAKE

1 Make the candied orange peel (see box, page 18) using the oranges, 200 g (6 ½ oz) of the sugar and the water. Reserve several pieces for decoration and finely chop the rest. Heat the oven to 180°C (350°F, Gas 4).

2 Butter, line and flour a 21 x 11 x 7.5-cm (8 ½ x 4 ½ x 3-inch) loaf tin (see box, page 17). Sift flour into a medium bowl with cocoa powder, baking powder and a pinch of salt.

Butter and sugar mixture will gradually lighten as sugar dissolves

3 With the electric mixer, cream the butter. Add the remaining 200 g (6 ½ oz) sugar and continue beating until light and fluffy, about 2-3 minutes.

4 Add the eggs to the butter and sugar mixture one by one, beating thoroughly with the electric mixer after each addition.

ANNE SAYS
'If the mixture begins to separate while adding the eggs, heat the bowl gently over hot water.'

Set bowl on dampened tea towel to hold it steady while you beat

Mix in candied peel
quickly and lightly

Rubber spatula
is ideal utensil

5 With the rubber spatula, stir the finely chopped candied orange peel evenly into the mixture.

6 Stir in the flour and cocoa powder mixture until just mixed.

7 Transfer the mixture to the prepared loaf tin. Tap the tin on the table to level the surface of the cake mixture and knock out large air bubbles.

Indentation in centre
is characteristic of
pound cake

8 Bake the pound cake in the heated oven until it shrinks slightly from the sides of the tin and the skewer inserted in the centre comes out clean, 50-60 minutes. While the cake is baking, make the orange icing (see page 17).

Metal skewer is used to
test if cake is done;
wooden cocktail stick
could also be used

HOW TO LINE AND FLOUR A LOAF TIN

Lining a cake tin with baking parchment keeps the cake from sticking to the inside of the tin. Flouring the tin also ensures that any excess butter will be absorbed from rich mixtures.

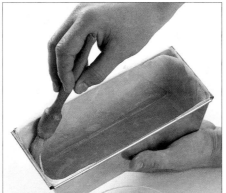

Tap side of tin so excess flour drops out

1 On the work surface, lay a rectangle of baking parchment 15 cm (6 inches) wider and 15 cm (6 inches) longer than the base of the loaf tin. Place the tin in the middle of the paper. With the scissors, snip diagonally from the corners of the paper to the corners of the tin.

2 Melt 30-45 ml (2-3 tbsp) of butter and brush the inside of the tin with an even coating, making sure that the bottom and top edges are covered. Press the paper into the tin, tucking in the overlaps to fit into the corners. Trim the paper even with the top edges. Butter the paper.

3 To flour the tin, sprinkle in 30-45 ml (2-3 tbsp) flour; turn the tin so the flour evenly coats the sides and bottom. Tap to remove excess.

2 MAKE THE ORANGE ICING

Hot water heats icing gently

Orange icing should have easy pouring consistency

1 Sift the icing sugar into a small bowl and stir in enough of the orange juice to make a soft paste.

ANNE SAYS
'Adjust the consistency of the icing by adding more icing sugar if the icing is too thin or more orange juice if it is too thick.'

2 Place the bowl in a saucepan of hot, not simmering, water, and heat until the icing is warm and will pour easily from the spoon. Keep the icing warm.

HOW TO MAKE CANDIED ORANGE PEEL

Fruits are candied, or crystallised, by being cooked in concentrated sugar syrup until translucent. Some fruits, in particular citrus peel and slices, can be candied at home easily. They make a tangy addition to cakes.

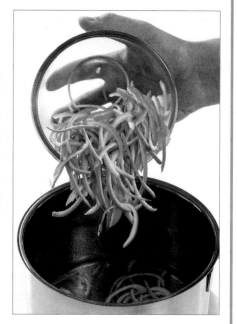

1 Score the orange peel lengthwise into quarters with a small knife, then strip away the peel and pith with your fingers.

ANNE SAYS
'Before peeling the oranges, roll them gently on the work surface to loosen the peel.'

2 Cut the peel into 5-mm (¼-inch) wide strips using a chef's knife.

3 Cut one orange in half and squeeze the juice; reserve for the icing.

4 Heat the sugar with the water in a saucepan until dissolved, then bring the syrup just to the boil. Put the strips of peel in the syrup.

Use slotted spoon to transfer peel from pan to rack

Put baking tray under rack to catch drips of syrup

5 Press a circle of baking parchment over the peel and weigh it down with a plate so the strips are immersed in syrup. Heat the syrup slowly to a simmer, taking 10-12 minutes, then poach until tender to the bite, about 1 hour.

6 Remove the pan from heat and allow the peel to soak in the syrup at room temperature 24 hours. Transfer peel to a rack placed over a tray; leave to dry, 3-5 hours.

3 ICE AND DECORATE THE CAKE

1 Remove the cake from the oven. Run the small knife round the sides of the warm cake to loosen it, then transfer it to the rack, with the baking tray below to catch the drips from the icing. Remove the baking parchment from the cake.

Pour icing slowly over cake to coat evenly

2 Pour the warm icing over the cake. Decorate the top with the reserved pieces of candied orange peel. Leave until the cake is cool and the icing has set.

🍽 **TO SERVE**
Transfer the cake to a serving plate and cut into thin slices.

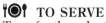

Pieces of candied orange peel make colourful contrast on top of dark brown cake

V A R I A T I O N

CHOCOLATE ORANGE MARBLE POUND CAKE

This attractive variation adds a swirl of plain orange mixture to Chocolate Orange Pound Cake.

1 Make the candied orange peel as directed, then chop all of it.
2 Sift the flour with the baking powder and salt and divide evenly between 2 bowls. Sift 45 ml (3 tbsp) cocoa powder into one of the bowls.
3 Continue making the cake mixture as directed in steps 3, 4 and 5, then divide it in half. Stir the cocoa mixture into one portion and the plain flour mixture into the other portion.
4 Pour the plain mixture into the prepared loaf tin.

5 Pour the chocolate mixture over the plain mixture in the tin.
6 Using the tip of a knife, swirl the mixtures together in a marbled pattern, taking care not to overmix them or the marbled effect will be lost.
7 Bake and ice the cake as directed.

CHOCOLATE MARBLE CHEESECAKE

🍽 SERVES 8-10   🥄 WORK TIME 35-40 MINUTES*   🍲 BAKING TIME 50-60 MINUTES

EQUIPMENT

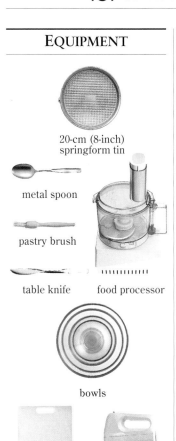

20-cm (8-inch) springform tin

metal spoon

pastry brush

table knife   food processor

bowls

chopping board

electric mixer

chef's knife

small knife

saucepans

rubber spatula

wooden spoon

INGREDIENTS

digestive biscuits

unsalted butter   plain chocolate

caster sugar

cream cheese   vanilla essence

eggs

This all-American favourite has swirls of plain and chocolate cheesecake fillings flavoured with vanilla in a crumbled biscuit base. The marbled filling is dense and rich, making it an ideal dinner party dessert.

GETTING AHEAD

The cheesecake can be made up to 3 days ahead and kept refrigerated; the flavour will mellow.

* plus 5-9 hours cooling and chilling time

metric	SHOPPING LIST	imperial
	For the biscuit base	
	melted butter for tin	
150 g	digestive biscuits	5 oz
75 g	unsalted butter	2 ½ oz
	For the cheesecake filling	
150 g	plain chocolate	5 oz
500 g	cream cheese, softened	1 lb
150 g	caster sugar	5 oz
5 ml	vanilla essence	1 tsp
2	eggs	2

ORDER OF WORK

1 MAKE THE BISCUIT BASE

2 MAKE THE CHEESECAKE FILLING

3 MARBLE AND BAKE THE CHEESECAKE

1 MAKE THE BISCUIT BASE

Brush melted butter thickly over side and bottom of tin

1 Generously brush the inside of the tin with melted butter and chill it.

Melted butter is best for brushing on inside of cake tin because it spreads evenly

2 Work the digestive biscuits to fine crumbs in the food processor; transfer to a bowl. Melt the butter in a small saucepan; add to the crumbs.

ANNE SAYS
'*As an alternative to working the biscuits to crumbs in a food processor, put them in a plastic bag and crush them with a rolling pin.*'

3 Stir with the wooden spoon until all the crumbs are moistened with melted butter.

Spread crushed biscuits evenly, pressing with back of metal spoon

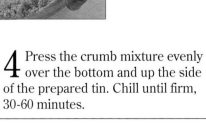

4 Press the crumb mixture evenly over the bottom and up the side of the prepared tin. Chill until firm, 30-60 minutes.

HOW TO MELT CHOCOLATE

Chocolate should be melted carefully because it may scorch or harden if overheated. It is also important that the container is uncovered and dry because any water or steam in contact with the chocolate may cause it to 'seize'. Once the chocolate begins to melt, stir it occasionally until completely melted and smooth, then remove it from the heat. There are a number of methods for melting chocolate. A double boiler is good; so, too, are the methods described here. Some cooks use a microwave oven: 60 g (2 oz) chopped plain chocolate takes about 2 minutes on Medium power, depending on the output.

Melt chopped chocolate in a glass bowl placed in a pan of hot, not simmering, water (a water bath).

Alternatively, spread chopped chocolate on an ovenproof plate and melt it over a pan of boiling water.

ANNE SAYS

'*If the chocolate 'seizes' during melting, stir in white vegetable fat or oil, 1 teaspoon at a time, until the chocolate is smooth again.*'

2 MAKE THE CHEESECAKE FILLING

1 Heat the oven to 180°C (350°F, Gas 4). Cut the chocolate into large chunks. Chop them with the chef's knife, or in the food processor using the pulse button. Melt the chocolate (see box, left) and allow to cool.

2 Beat the cream cheese until smooth with the electric mixer, 2-3 minutes, or you can use the wooden spoon. Add the sugar and vanilla essence and beat just until smooth.

3 Add the eggs one by one, beating well after each addition.

Beat one egg in thoroughly before adding next

4 Pour half of the filling into the biscuit base.

5 Mix the cooled melted chocolate into the remaining filling.

3 MARBLE AND BAKE THE CHEESECAKE

1 Slowly spoon a ring of the chocolate filling over the plain filling.

2 Using the table knife, swirl the fillings together to make a marbled pattern. Take care not to over-mix or the marbled effect will be lost. Bake the cheesecake in the heated oven until the side is set but the centre remains soft, 50-60 minutes. Turn off the oven and leave the cheesecake in the cooling-down oven until completely cool. Refrigerate at least 4 hours.

ANNE SAYS
'It is important to cool the cheesecake slowly in the oven or it will crack.'

Chocolate and vanilla fillings are swirled together to create marbled effect

Slowly draw chocolate filling in from edge to centre to create swirled effect

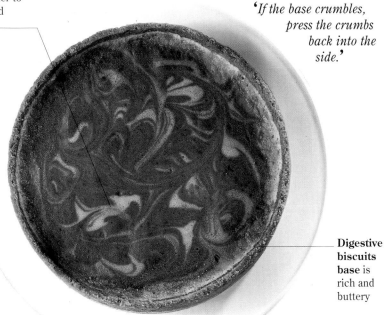

🍴 TO SERVE
Run the small knife round the side of the cheesecake to loosen it, remove the tin and transfer the cheesecake to a serving plate.

ANNE SAYS
'If the base crumbles, press the crumbs back into the side.'

Digestive biscuits base is rich and buttery

ALL-CHOCOLATE CHEESECAKE

A thoroughly chocolate version of Chocolate Marble Cheesecake.

1 Make the base as directed.
2 Chop and melt 300 g (10 oz) plain chocolate.
3 Prepare the filling as directed, using only 100 g (3 ½ oz) sugar and stirring in cooled, melted chocolate after eggs.
4 Pour the filling into the prepared base and bake as directed.

WHITE CHOCOLATE CHEESECAKE

Another version of Chocolate Marble Cheesecake – all in white.

1 Make the base as directed.
2 Chop and melt 250 g (8 oz) white chocolate.
3 Prepare the filling as directed, using only 100 g (3 ½ oz) sugar and stirring in cooled, melted chocolate after eggs.
4 Pour the filling into the prepared base and bake as directed.

SPECKLED CHOCOLATE CAKE

¡❍¡ SERVES 8 ⇥ WORK TIME 30-35 MINUTES* ☕ BAKING TIME ABOUT 60 MINUTES

EQUIPMENT

electric mixer

20-cm (8-inch) round cake tin

small knife

chef's knife**

kitchen scissors

bowls

saucepan

vegetable peeler

pastry brush

whisk

sieves

palette knife

wooden spoon

rubber spatula

tea towel

wire rack

thin card

baking parchment

**food processor can also be used

This moist cake, laden with little pieces of chocolate, was created by master French Chef Fernand Point. The chopped chocolate should be slightly granular and a food processor gives the ideal texture, or use a chef's knife.

GETTING AHEAD
The cake keeps well in an airtight container up to 3 days. Frost it not more than 2 hours before serving.

* plus cooling time

metric	SHOPPING LIST	imperial
	For the cake mixture	
	butter for tin	
125 g	unsalted butter	4 oz
4	eggs	4
250 g	caster sugar	8 oz
125 g	plain chocolate	4 oz
125 g	plain flour	4 oz
	For the chocolate frosting	
175 g	bittersweet chocolate	6 oz
175 g	butter	6 oz
175 g	icing sugar	6 oz
	To finish	
1	bar plain chocolate	1
	icing sugar	

INGREDIENTS

plain and bittersweet chocolate

eggs

icing sugar

butter

flour

caster sugar

chocolate bar

ORDER OF WORK

1 MAKE THE CAKE MIXTURE

2 BAKE THE CAKE

3 MAKE THE CHOCOLATE FROSTING

4 FINISH THE CAKE

1 MAKE THE CAKE MIXTURE

1 Heat the oven to 180°C (350°F, Gas 4). Butter the cake tin and line the bottom with baking parchment. Butter the paper. Put the unsalted butter in a small bowl and place it in the saucepan half filled with hot water.

2 Warm the butter, stirring occasionally, until it is soft enough to pour. Remove from the heat and allow to cool slightly.

Warmed butter should be pourable but not oily

Gradually add sugar to egg yolks while beating with electric mixer

3 Separate the eggs. Beat the egg yolks with about two-thirds of the sugar until light and the mixture leaves a ribbon trail when the beaters are lifted, 3-5 minutes.

4 In a separate bowl, whisk the egg whites until stiff. Sprinkle in the remaining sugar and continue whisking until glossy to make a light meringue, about 20 seconds.

Lift egg yolk mixture up and over chopped chocolate until speckled

5 Add the softened butter to the egg yolk mixture and stir in gently.

6 Cut the chocolate into large chunks. Chop them with the chef's knife, or in a food processor using the pulse button.

7 Stir the chopped chocolate into the egg yolk mixture.

8 Sift about one-third of the flour into the chocolate mixture. Add about one-third of the meringue and fold them together as lightly as possible.

Use rubber spatula to fold mixtures gently together

9 Add the remaining flour and meringue in the same way in 2 more batches.

ANNE SAYS
'If the ingredients are folded together gently, air will be retained in the mixture and the finished cake will be light.'

2 BAKE THE CAKE

1 Spoon the cake mixture into the prepared tin. Bake the cake in the heated oven until it has shrunk slightly from the side of the tin, about 60 minutes.

After turning mixture into cake tin, tap tin on work surface so top of mixture is level

2 Remove the cake from the oven. Run the small knife round the edge of the cake to loosen it from the tin.

ANNE SAYS
'It can be hard to tell when the cake is done because the crisp top will be cracked and will not spring back when pressed with a fingertip. If in doubt, leave it in the oven longer.'

3 Place the wire rack on top of the cake and then turn both over together to unmould the cake.

Base of cake tin will be hot, so protect your hand with tea towel or oven glove

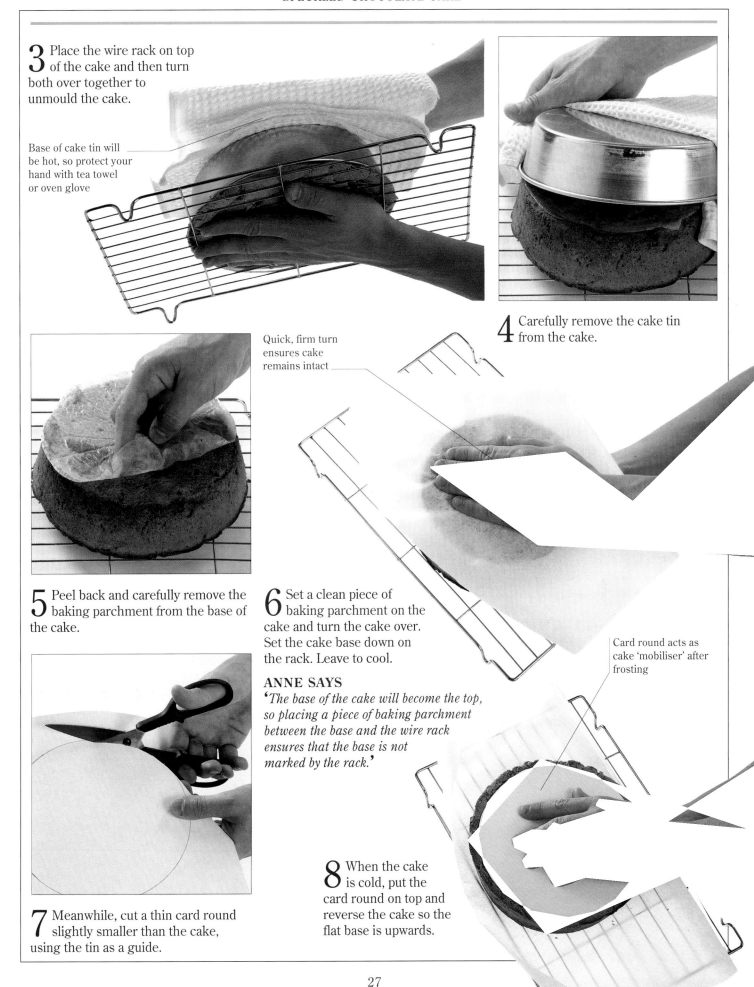

4 Carefully remove the cake tin from the cake.

Quick, firm turn ensures cake remains intact

5 Peel back and carefully remove the baking parchment from the base of the cake.

6 Set a clean piece of baking parchment on the cake and turn the cake over. Set the cake base down on the rack. Leave to cool.

ANNE SAYS
'*The base of the cake will become the top, so placing a piece of baking parchment between the base and the wire rack ensures that the base is not marked by the rack.*'

Card round acts as cake 'mobiliser' after frosting

7 Meanwhile, cut a thin card round slightly smaller than the cake, using the tin as a guide.

8 When the cake is cold, put the card round on top and reverse the cake so the flat base is upwards.

3 MAKE THE CHOCOLATE FROSTING

1 Chop the chocolate and melt it in a bowl placed in the pan of hot water until melted. Allow to cool slightly.

2 Meanwhile, using the wooden spoon, work the butter until it becomes soft and smooth.

3 Sift the icing sugar and add it to the softened butter.

4 Beat the mixture well until it becomes light and creamy.

HOW TO MAKE CHOCOLATE CURLS

It is easiest to form curls from a bar of chocolate, although only a small portion of the bar may be needed. Covering chocolate (couverture), plain, milk or white chocolate can all be used, whichever you prefer.

The chocolate should be at room temperature (about 21°C/70°F). Holding the bar at an angle, use a vegetable peeler to shave curls from the edge on to baking parchment.

Whisk quickly in warm place to keep chocolate fluid

Folded damp tea towel placed underneath bowl will prevent skidding

5 Add the melted chocolate to the creamy butter and sugar mixture, whisking quickly as you pour in the chocolate.

ANNE SAYS
'Prepare the frosting in a warm place because it sets quickly.'

6 Pour about half of the frosting on top of the cake and spread it evenly over the top and side with the palette knife. Dip the knife in hot water, dry it quickly and smooth the top and side of the cake.

4 FINISH THE CAKE

1 Make the chocolate curls using the bar of plain chocolate (see box, page 28). Using the palette knife, lift the curls and sprinkle them on top of the cake.

Tap knife to release any curls that stick

2 Sift icing sugar evenly over the chocolate curls. Transfer the cake to a serving plate.

Chocolate curls are a simple but effective garnish

Chocolate frosting covers any unevenness in cake

V A R I A T I O N

CHOCOLATE BUTTERFLY CAKES

Hollowed cakes are filled with chocolate frosting and the tops are split to form 'wings'. Children love to make these small speckled chocolate cakes take flight.

1 Line 12-hole bun tin with paper cake cases. Prepare the cake mixture as directed, adding 2.5 ml ($1/2$ tsp) baking powder to the flour. Spoon into cake cases, filling them three-quarters full. Bake the cakes until firm to the touch, 15-20 minutes. Remove from the oven, lift out of bun tin and place on a wire rack; allow to cool.
2 Make the chocolate frosting.

3 With a small knife, slice a deep cone from each of the cakes and cut each cone in half. Fill the hollows with the frosting, using a piping bag and star nozzle if you like. Arrange the cut halves on top to resemble butterfly wings. Sift over a little icing sugar just before serving.

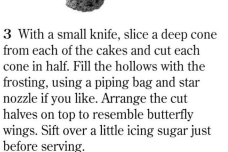

SACHERTORTE

EQUIPMENT

bowls

sieve

small knife

teaspoon

chef's knife

palette knife

whisk

scissors

pastry brush

baking tray

conical sieve

wire rack

25-cm (10-inch) round cake tin

saucepans

baking parchment

sugar thermometer

chopping board

wooden spoon**

rubber spatula

**electric mixer can also be used

The world-famous chocolate cake from Sacher's pastry shop in Vienna is embossed with the name 'Sacher', which accounts for its renown.

GETTING AHEAD
The cake can be baked, iced and stored up to 1 week in an airtight container.

* plus cooling time

metric	SHOPPING LIST	imperial
	For the chocolate cake	
	butter and flour for tin	
125 g	plain chocolate	4 oz
6	eggs	6
125 g	unsalted butter	4 oz
135 g	icing sugar	4 ½ oz
2.5 ml	vanilla essence	½ tsp
100 g	caster sugar	3 ½ oz
100 g	plain flour	3 ½ oz
	For the apricot jam glaze	
175 g	apricot jam	6 oz
45-60 ml	water	3-4 tbsp
	For the chocolate icing	
250 g	bittersweet chocolate	8 oz
250 g	caster sugar	8 oz
125 ml	water	4 fl oz

INGREDIENTS

eggs

plain and bittersweet chocolate

icing sugar

unsalted butter

apricot jam

vanilla essence

caster sugar

plain flour

ORDER OF WORK

1   PREPARE AND BAKE THE CHOCOLATE CAKE

2   MAKE THE APRICOT JAM GLAZE; USE TO COAT THE CAKE

3   MAKE THE CHOCOLATE ICING AND ICE THE CAKE

1 PREPARE AND BAKE THE CHOCOLATE CAKE

1 Heat the oven to 180°C (350°F, Gas 4). Butter the cake tin, line the bottom with baking parchment, butter the parchment and flour the tin. Cut the chocolate into large chunks. Chop them with the chef's knife, or in a food processor using the pulse button. Melt in a bowl placed in a saucepan with hot water.

Stir chocolate with rubber spatula while it melts to ensure smooth texture

2 Separate the eggs. With the wooden spoon, cream the butter. Add the icing sugar and vanilla essence and continue beating until light and fluffy, 2-3 minutes.

Steady bowl with other hand while beating

3 Add the egg yolks one by one, beating well after each addition. Stir in the melted chocolate.

Use wooden spoon to beat melted chocolate thoroughly into egg yolk and sugar mixture

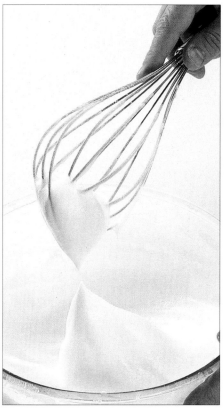

4 Whisk the egg whites until stiff. Sprinkle in the caster sugar and continue whisking until glossy to make a light meringue, about 20 seconds.

5 Sift about one-third of the flour over the chocolate mixture, add about one-third of the meringue, and fold together as lightly as possible, using the rubber spatula.

Use rubber spatula for folding meringue into flour and chocolate mixture

When folding, turn bowl anti-clockwise

6 Add the remaining flour and the remaining meringue in the same way, in 2 batches, and fold together as lightly as possible. Cut down into the centre of the bowl with the rubber spatula, scoop under the contents and turn them over in a rolling motion.

7 Pour the chocolate cake mixture into the prepared cake tin.

Use rubber spatula to scrape every last bit of mixture from bowl

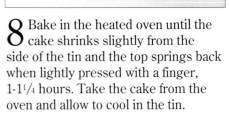

8 Bake in the heated oven until the cake shrinks slightly from the side of the tin and the top springs back when lightly pressed with a finger, 1-1¼ hours. Take the cake from the oven and allow to cool in the tin.

2 MAKE THE APRICOT JAM GLAZE; USE TO COAT THE CAKE

1 With scissors, trim a piece of thin card into a round slightly smaller than the cake. Make a jam glaze with the apricot jam (see box, right). Run the small knife round the edge of the cooled cake.

2 Set the card round on the cake, then invert the cake on to the wire rack. Set the rack with the baking tray below to catch the drips from the glaze. Remove the paper.

Invert cake on to rack so cake turns out upside-down on card and base becomes top

3 Brush top and side of the cake with the warm apricot jam glaze.

ANNE SAYS
'*Be generous with the glaze because it adds moisture to the cake.*'

HOW TO MAKE JAM GLAZE

Fruit jam glaze is spread on cakes to help keep them moist It can also complement cake flavours.

Melt the jam with the water in a small saucepan. Work it through a conical sieve into a bowl, then return it to the saucepan and melt it again over low heat.

Brush glaze evenly over top and side of cake

33

HOW TO MAKE A PAPER PIPING CONE

Disposable paper piping cones are useful for small amounts of icing or filling to be piped with a plain nozzle. You can also make a large piping cone and use it in place of a nylon piping bag, snipping a larger opening in the end and dropping in a piping nozzle.

   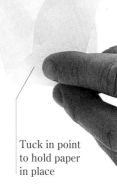

Tuck in point
to hold paper
in place

1 Fold a 20 x 35-cm (8 x 14-inch) piece of baking parchment diagonally in half from corner to corner; cut along fold.

2 Fold the short side of one triangle over to the right-angled corner to form a cone shape.

3 Holding the cone together with one hand, wrap the long point of the triangle around the paper cone with the other hand.

4 Tuck the point of paper inside the cone to secure it. (The remaining triangle of paper can be used for another cone.)

3 MAKE THE CHOCOLATE ICING AND ICE THE CAKE

1 Cut the bittersweet chocolate into large chunks. Chop them with the chef's knife, or in a food processor using the pulse button.

Work melted
chocolate from
side to side in
sweeping motion

2 In a saucepan, melt the chocolate, sugar and water, stirring. Continue heating to 93.5°C (200°F) on the sugar thermometer, stirring, then pour on to a marble or laminate work surface. Cool slightly.

3 With the palette knife, work the mixture vigorously until it cools and thickens to a smooth and shiny consistency, 5-7 minutes.

Pour and spread icing quickly before it sets

Smooth bumps with palette knife dipped in hot water

4 When the icing is firm, return it to the saucepan and heat gently until melted and lukewarm. Pour about three-quarters of the icing as quickly as possible on the top of the cake and spread it over the top and side with the palette knife. Smooth the side, patching gaps with more icing.

! TAKE CARE !
When heating the icing, do not let it get too hot or it will lose its gloss. If necessary to thin it, add a very little water. It must coat a spoon.

ANNE SAYS
'*Use both hands to steady paper piping cone while piping.*'

5 Transfer the cake to a serving plate. Make a paper piping cone (see box, page 34). Fill the cone with the remaining icing, using the teaspoon. Fold the top to seal and trim the tip. Pipe 'Sacher' on top of the cake.

'Sacher' is perfectly piped with chocolate icing

Chocolate icing is smooth and glossy

V A R I A T I O N

CHOCOLATE RASPBERRY TORTE

Changing the apricot glaze to raspberry gives Sachertorte a surprising twist.

1 Prepare and bake the chocolate cake as directed; allow to cool.
2 Make a jam glaze (see box, page 33), using raspberry jam; use to cover the cake.
3 Ice the cake as directed.
4 If you like, in place of piping the 'Sacher' on top, pipe a more simple design, or leave the top of the cake plain if you prefer.
5 Serve with fresh raspberries and whipped cream.

BLACK FOREST CAKE

Schwarzwalder Kirschtorte

🍽️ SERVES 8-10 🥣 WORK TIME 45-50 MINUTES* 🍲 BAKING TIME 35-40 MINUTES

EQUIPMENT

chef's knife

pastry brush

scissors

food processor

cherry stoner   bowls

large serrated knife

rubber spatula

wire rack

whisk

grater

saucepans

sieve

wooden spoon

palette knife

baking parchment

plate

piping bag and
medium nozzle

20-cm (8-inch)
springform tin

8-10 rose leaves

*Few commercial versions approach the quality of
a Black Forest cake made at home. Rye bread
crumbs are used in the mixture, and the cake is
filled with cherries and cream.*

* plus cooling time

INGREDIENTS

black
cherries

plain
chocolate

cocoa powder

kirsch

whole blanched
almonds

dark rye bread

eggs

double cream

flour

unsalted butter

baking powder

sugar

metric	SHOPPING LIST	imperial
	For the cake mixture	
3-4	slices of dark rye bread, about 250 g (8 oz)	3-4
75 g	unsalted butter + extra for tin	2 1/2 oz
60 g	plain flour + extra for tin	2 oz
2.5 ml	baking powder	1/2 tsp
30 ml	cocoa powder	2 tbsp
60 g	plain chocolate	2 oz
90 g	whole blanched almonds	3 oz
4	eggs	4
100 g	caster sugar	3 1/2 oz
15 ml	kirsch	1 tbsp
15 ml	water	1 tbsp
	For the filling and decoration	
180 g	plain chocolate	6 oz
350 g	black cherries, fresh or canned in syrup	12 oz
	For the Chantilly cream	
500 ml	double cream	16 fl oz
30 ml	caster sugar	2 tbsp
30 ml	kirsch	2 tbsp
	For the kirsch syrup	
60 g	granulated sugar	2 oz
125 ml	water	4 fl oz
30 ml	kirsch	2 tbsp

ORDER OF WORK

1. **PREPARE AND BAKE THE CAKE**

2. **PREPARE THE FILLING AND DECORATION**

3. **SLICE THE CAKE HORIZONTALLY INTO 3 LAYERS**

4. **ASSEMBLE THE CAKE**

1 PREPARE AND BAKE THE CAKE

1 Heat the oven to 180°C (350°F, Gas 4). Butter the cake tin, line the bottom with baking parchment, butter the parchment and flour the tin.

2 Discard the crusts from the bread. Blend the bread to fine crumbs in the food processor or in a blender. Melt the butter and leave to cool.

Cut slices of bread in half if necessary to fit into feed tube

3 Sift the flour, baking powder and cocoa powder into a bowl. Cut the chocolate into large chunks. Chop them in the food processor or with the chef's knife. Add to the bowl with the breadcrumbs. Stir to mix. Finely grind the almonds in the food processor.

Use large balloon whisk or electric mixer to beat egg yolks and sugar

4 Separate the eggs. In a large bowl, beat the egg yolks with half of the sugar until the mixture is very thick and light in colour, about 5 minutes.

5 Add the almonds, kirsch and water and stir in with the wooden spoon. Set aside.

6 Whisk the egg whites until stiff. Sprinkle in the remaining sugar and continue whisking until glossy to form a light meringue, about 20 seconds. Add about one-third to the yolk mixture and fold together lightly.

7 Fold the chocolate and bread-crumb mixture into the egg mixture in 3 batches.

Rubber spatula will scrape all meringue from bowl

8 Fold in the remaining meringue with the rubber spatula, scooping under the contents and turning them over in a rolling motion.

9 Pour the melted, cooled butter into the chocolate and egg mixture and fold in gently.

10 Pour the mixture into the prepared cake tin. Bake the cake in the heated oven until it shrinks slightly from the side of the tin and the top springs back when lightly pressed with a fingertip, 35-40 minutes.

11 Run a knife round the side of the cake to loosen it, then release the side of the tin. Transfer the cake to the wire rack, placing it upside-down on a piece of baking parchment. Remove the tin base, peel off the lining paper and allow the cake to cool. Meanwhile, prepare the filling and decoration.

Baking parchment peels off easily from bottom of cake and does not stick

2 PREPARE THE FILLING AND DECORATION

1 Make the chocolate leaves: melt 90 g (3 oz) of the chocolate in a bowl placed in a saucepan half-filled with hot water; brush the chocolate on the shiny side of each rose leaf in a thin, even layer, leaving a little of the stem exposed. Place the leaves on the plate and allow to cool, then refrigerate until the chocolate has set. Carefully peel leaves away from chocolate.

2 Make the Chantilly cream: pour the cream into a bowl placed in a larger bowl of iced water and whip until soft peaks form. Add the sugar and kirsch and continue whipping until stiff peaks form. Coarsely grate 60 g (2 oz) of the remaining chocolate (see box, right).

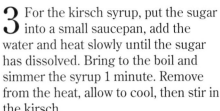

3 For the kirsch syrup, put the sugar into a small saucepan, add the water and heat slowly until the sugar has dissolved. Bring to the boil and simmer the syrup 1 minute. Remove from the heat, allow to cool, then stir in the kirsch.

4 Reserve 8-10 cherries, with stems, for the decoration. Stone the remaining cherries. If using canned cherries, drain them.

Cherry stoner removes stones neatly

Choose 8-10 perfect cherries with stems attached for decoration

HOW TO GRATE CHOCOLATE

Grated chocolate makes a simple, attractive garnish for cakes and desserts. It is important that the chocolate should be firm, so chill it before grating.

If the chocolate is in one large piece, first break it into smaller pieces. When grating, hold the piece of chocolate with a piece of baking parchment or foil to keep it from melting in your hand. Work the chocolate against the largest grid of a grater to obtain coarse chocolate shavings.

5 Melt the remaining 30 g (1 oz) chocolate. Dip the cherries with stems into the chocolate to coat evenly. Set the coated cherries on baking parchment and leave them to cool.

3 SLICE THE CAKE HORIZONTALLY INTO 3 LAYERS

Vertical cut makes sliced layers easy to line up when reassembling cake so it will be even

Hold hand firmly on top of cake to guide knife

1 If necessary, trim any crusty edges from the cake. With scissors, cut 2 rounds of thin card slightly smaller than the cake; set the cake on top of one round. With the point of the chef's knife, make a small vertical cut in the side of the cake. Using the serrated knife, cut the cake horizontally into 3 even layers.

2 Turn the cake, not the knife, as you cut the layers with an even, broad slicing motion.

4 ASSEMBLE THE CAKE

Use palette knife to spread cream gently over cherries

1 Brush the cooled kirsch syrup evenly on each of the cake layers to moisten.

2 Spread the bottom cake layer with one-eighth of the Chantilly cream. Top with half of the stoned cherries. Spread with another one-eighth cream.

3 Lift the middle cake layer with the second round of card, place it on the bottom layer and press down lightly. Brush with more kirsch syrup.

Slide round of card from under cake layer as it is set over cream and cherries

4 Fill the second layer in the same way as the first, using another one-quarter of the remaining Chantilly cream and the remaining cherries.

5 Set the top cake layer in place, cut-side down. Transfer the cake on the card to a bowl or cake stand.

With fingers, gently press top cake layer into cream so it will sit firmly on cake

6 Neaten the side of the cake by smoothing any cream that has pressed out between the layers.

Grated chocolate is handled easily with baking parchment

Plate underneath cake catches grated chocolate as it falls

7 Spread half of the remaining Chantilly cream smoothly over the top and side of the cake.

8 Press the grated chocolate around the side, using a piece of baking parchment to help.

9 Transfer the cake to a serving plate. Mark a lattice on top of the cake with the edge of the palette knife.

Hold palette knife at right angles to cake

Gently press edge of knife into cream to make thin grooves

10 Put the remaining Chantilly cream into the piping bag with the medium star nozzle and pipe rosettes round the top edge of the cake.

When piping rosettes, hold piping bag upright and squeeze gently

🍽 **TO SERVE**
Top the rosettes with the chocolate-dipped cherries and add the chocolate leaves.

Cherry and Chantilly cream filling is revealed when cake is sliced

BLACK FOREST STRIP CAKE

1 Prepare the cake mixture as directed in the main recipe.
2 In place of the springform cake tin, butter a large baking sheet, line it with baking parchment, and butter the parchment. Spread the mixture on the baking sheet in a 30 x 37-cm (12 x 15-inch) rectangle.
3 Bake the cake until the top springs back when pressed with a fingertip, 5-10 minutes.
4 Trim the crusty edges from the cake and cut it lengthwise into 3 equal strips.
5 Fill and layer the cake strips as directed.
6 To decorate, pipe the remaining Chantilly cream on top using a plain nozzle and sprinkle lightly with grated chocolate. Omit the chocolate leaves and chocolate-coated cherries if you like.

GETTING AHEAD
The cake can be baked 3 days ahead and stored in an airtight container. After filling, it can be kept, covered, in the refrigerator 12-24 hours and the flavours will mellow. The chocolate leaves can be layered with baking parchment and stored in the refrigerator up to 1 week. Assemble the cake not more than 2 hours before serving.

HOW TO MAKE AND CRUSH PRALINE

Praline is made by caramelising equal weights of sugar and whole unblanched almonds directly over low heat. The nuts should be thoroughly toasted to develop their flavour. Praline can be kept several weeks in an airtight container at room temperature. It can also be frozen.

1 Lightly brush a baking sheet or marble slab with oil. Combine the nuts and sugar in a heavy-based saucepan. Heat gently until the sugar melts, stirring often with a wooden spoon. Continue cooking over fairly low heat to a medium caramel, stirring lightly. The sugar should be a deep golden brown and the almonds should make a popping sound, showing that they are toasted.

2 Remove the pan from the heat and immediately pour the sugar mixture on to the oiled baking sheet or marble slab. Spread out the praline with the wooden spoon and leave it until cool and crisp, 10-15 minutes.

! TAKE CARE !
The mixture is very hot when pouring it from the pan on to the baking sheet.

3 To crush the praline: crack the praline into pieces with a rolling pin, then grind to the desired consistency in a food processor or blender. For a more even texture, grind the praline in 3 or 4 batches.

ANNE SAYS
'For large chunks of praline, put the praline in a thick plastic bag and pound it into pieces with a rolling pin.'

V A R I A T I O N

CHOCOLATE PRALINE CAKE

Crunchy praline made with toasted almonds and caramel replaces the cherries in Black Forest Cake. Use rum for flavouring the syrup instead of kirsch. The cake is best served the day it is made.

1 Prepare and bake the cake as directed.
2 Make praline (see box, left), using 150 g (5 oz) whole unblanched almonds and 150 g (5 oz) sugar, and separating 8-10 whole caramel-coated almonds for the garnish. When the sheet of praline has set, crush it finely.
3 Make the Chantilly cream.
4 Mix two-thirds of the finely crushed praline into two-thirds of the Chantilly cream. Use the cream for filling, reserving enough to decorate the top.
5 Assemble the cake as directed, omitting the cherries and grated chocolate.
6 Cover the top and side of the cake with the plain Chantilly cream. Omit the lattice.
7 Press the remaining praline round the side and pipe rosettes of the reserved praline Chantilly cream in a ring on top of the cake.
8 Garnish with the caramel-coated almonds.

CHOCOLATE CHESTNUT ROLL

 SERVES 8-10   WORK TIME 50-55 MINUTES   BAKING TIME 5-7 MINUTES

EQUIPMENT

whisk*

chef's knife

serrated knife

saucepans

plain tea towel or large napkin

piping bag and small star nozzle

rose leaves

palette knife

baking parchment

wooden spoon

sieve

plate

chopping board

pastry brush

baking sheets

rubber spatula

*electric mixer can also be used

INGREDIENTS

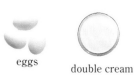

eggs   double cream

flour

chestnut purée   marrons glacés

cocoa powder

plain chocolate   dark rum

caster sugar

A winter favourite, especially over the Christmas period, this rolled sponge cake is filled with a rich chestnut purée mixed with whipped cream. Decorated with piped cream, marrons glacés and delicate chocolate leaves, it looks superb.

GETTING AHEAD

Once the cake is assembled, it will keep 1-2 days in the refrigerator. Add the cream decoration, marrons glacés and chocolate leaves just before serving.

metric	SHOPPING LIST	imperial
	For the chocolate sponge roll	
	butter for baking sheet	
35 g	cocoa powder	1 1/4 oz
15 ml	plain flour	1 tbsp
	salt	
5	eggs	5
150 g	caster sugar	5 oz
	For the filling	
175 ml	double cream	6 fl oz
125 g	chestnut purée	4 oz
30 ml	dark rum	2 tbsp
30 g	plain chocolate	1 oz
	caster sugar to taste (optional)	
	To finish and decorate	
90 g	plain chocolate for chocolate leaves	3 oz
50 g	caster sugar	1 3/4 oz
60 ml	water	2 fl oz
30 ml	dark rum	2 tbsp
125 ml	double cream	4 fl oz
8-10	marrons glacés	8-10

ORDER OF WORK

1 MAKE THE CHOCOLATE CAKE MIXTURE

2 BAKE, TURN OUT, AND ROLL THE SPONGE

3 MAKE THE FILLING

4 FINISH AND DECORATE THE CAKE

1 MAKE THE CHOCOLATE CAKE MIXTURE

1 Heat the oven to 220°C (425°F, Gas 7). Brush a 30 x 37-cm (12 x 15-inch) baking sheet with melted butter, line with baking parchment and butter the paper.

Be sure to cover entire surface of baking sheet

Melted butter is easy to brush on evenly

2 Sift the cocoa powder, flour and a pinch of salt into a bowl.

Colour of egg yolk mixture will lighten as you whisk

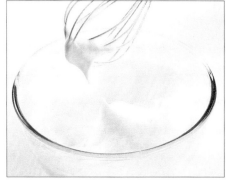

3 Separate the eggs. Beat the egg yolks with two-thirds of the sugar until light, and the mixture leaves a ribbon trail when the whisk is lifted, about 3-5 minutes.

4 Whisk the egg whites until stiff. Sprinkle in the remaining sugar and continue whisking until glossy to make a light meringue, about 20 seconds.

ANNE SAYS
'Your bowl and whisk must be completely free of any trace of water, grease or egg yolk or the egg whites will not whisk to full volume.'

When folding, cut down through mixture and move spatula down and around; turn bowl anti-clockwise with other hand

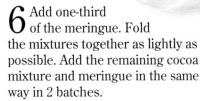

5 Sift about one-third of the cocoa mixture over the egg-yolk mixture.

ANNE SAYS
'Double sifting ensures the cocoa powder will be evenly distributed.'

6 Add one-third of the meringue. Fold the mixtures together as lightly as possible. Add the remaining cocoa mixture and meringue in the same way in 2 batches.

2 | **BAKE, TURN OUT, AND ROLL THE SPONGE**

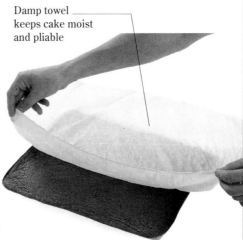

Damp towel
keeps cake moist
and pliable

1 Pour the chocolate mixture, all at once, on to the prepared baking sheet. Use the rubber spatula to scrape out the bowl.

2 Spread the mixture evenly on the baking sheet almost to the edges. Put in the heated oven, near the bottom, and bake about 5-7 minutes. The cake is done when it is risen and just firm to the touch. Do not overbake the cake or it will be difficult to roll.

3 Dampen the tea towel. Remove the cake from the oven and immediately cover with the tea towel.

4 Take a second baking sheet and set it on top of the cake. Quickly invert the cake so the original baking sheet is on top. Place the cake on the work surface and carefully remove the uppermost baking sheet.

Put second baking
sheet on top of damp
towel so cake can be
turned over easily

Using even pressure,
roll down length
from short end

5 Holding the baking parchment by its edges, carefully peel it off the cake.

6 Starting at the short end nearest you, fold over the end of the towel so it overlaps the cake and then tightly roll up the cake lengthwise. Set aside to cool.

3 MAKE THE FILLING

Rubber spatula is ideal for folding mixtures

1 Pour the cream into a chilled bowl and whip until it forms soft peaks and just holds a shape.

ANNE SAYS
'Set the chilled bowl in a larger one filled with iced water. This helps keep cream chilled, and is especially effective in hot weather.'

2 Put the chestnut purée in another bowl and add the rum; this will soften the purée. Cut the chocolate into large chunks, then chop with the chef's knife, or in a food processor. Melt the chocolate in a bowl placed in a saucepan half-filled with hot water. Add to the chestnut purée and stir well with the wooden spoon to remove any lumps.

3 Stir about 30 ml (2 tbsp) of the whipped cream into the mixture to soften it, then fold the chocolate and chestnut mixture into the rest of the whipped cream. If necessary, add sugar to taste.

4 FINISH AND DECORATE THE CAKE

Carefully unroll cooled cake

1 Use the 90 g (3 oz) plain chocolate to make 8-10 chocolate leaves (see box, page 48). Reserve for the decoration.

2 Make a rum syrup: in a small saucepan, over low heat, heat half of the sugar in the water until it dissolves. Simmer the syrup 1 minute. Allow to cool, then stir in the rum.

3 Unroll the cake, then roll it up again without the towel. Place the cake on a sheet of baking parchment and unroll it. The smooth top will be on the outside when rolled.

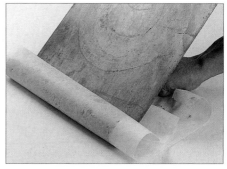

4 Brush the top of the cake with the cooled rum syrup. Using the palette knife, spread the chestnut filling evenly over the top.

5 Using the paper underneath, carefully roll up the filled cake as tightly as possible.

6 Bring the paper up over the cake; fold it in tightly. Insert the edge of the baking sheet against the fold and push away from you to tighten the roll.

HOW TO MAKE CHOCOLATE LEAVES

If melted chocolate is brushed on leaves and left to set, the original leaves can be peeled off, leaving chocolate facsimiles. Pliable leaves with deep veins, such as rose, are best. Chocolate leaves can be layered with baking parchment and then stored in the refrigerator up to 1 week.

1 Cut the chocolate into large chunks. Chop them with a chef's knife, or in a food processor using the pulse button. Melt the chocolate in a bowl placed in a saucepan half-filled with hot water. For a shiny finish on the leaves, temper the chocolate (see page 55). Using a pastry brush or your fingertip, spread chocolate on the shiny side of each leaf in a thin even layer, leaving a little of the stem exposed so it is easy to peel off the leaf. Place the leaves on a plate and allow to cool; refrigerate until set.

2 With the tips of your fingers, peel the leaves away from the chocolate, handling as little as possible so it does not melt and become dull.

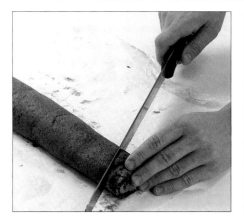

7 With the serrated knife, cut each end of the cake on the diagonal. Transfer the cake to a serving plate for decorating.

8 Pour the cream into a chilled bowl and whip until soft peaks form. Add the remaining sugar and continue whipping until stiff peaks form and the whisk leaves clear marks. Fill the piping bag with the cream.

9 Pipe a continuous wavy line of whipped cream over the rolled cake. Arrange the chocolate leaves and marrons glacés along each side of the roll.

Hold piping bag steady so waves of cream are even

Star nozzle creates delicate piped decoration

Piped whipped cream adds interest to plain top of rolled cake

Marrons glacés alternate with chocolate leaves

CHOCOLATE STRAWBERRY CREAM CAKE

This cake has a lighter filling than that in the main recipe. With its strawberry sauce, it is ideal for summer occasions.

1 Make and roll up the chocolate sponge as directed.
2 Whip 175 ml (6 fl oz) double cream with 30 ml (2 tbsp) sugar. Fold 250 g (8 oz) chopped strawberries into the cream.
3 Make the sugar syrup, using kirsch instead of rum, and brush over the cake.
4 Fill and roll up the cake as directed.
5 Dip fresh strawberries in melted chocolate and leave to set on baking parchment.

6 Meanwhile, make a strawberry coulis: hull 500 g (1 lb) strawberries, washing them only if dirty. Purée the strawberries in a food processor. Stir in 30 ml (2 tbsp) kirsch (optional) and 30-45 ml (2-3 tbsp) icing sugar to taste.
7 Slice the cake and arrange on individual plates with pools of strawberry coulis. Decorate with chocolate-dipped strawberries.

CHOCOLATE NUT CREAM CAKE WITH CARAMEL SAUCE

This version has a filling of crunchy praline and a creamy caramel sauce.

1 Make and roll up the chocolate sponge as directed.
2 Make praline: lightly brush a baking sheet or marble slab with oil. Heat 100 g (3 1/2 oz) unblanched hazelnuts and 100 g (3 1/2 oz) sugar in a heavy-based saucepan until the sugar melts, stirring often with a wooden spoon. Continue cooking over fairly low heat to a medium caramel, stirring lightly. The sugar should be a deep golden brown and the hazelnuts should make a popping sound.
3 Immediately pour the mixture on to the oiled baking sheet or marble slab. Spread out the praline with the wooden spoon and leave until cool and crisp, 10-15 minutes.
4 Reserve some whole hazelnuts coated with caramel for decoration. Crack the remainder into pieces with a rolling pin, then coarsely grind in a food processor or blender.
5 Whip 175 ml (6 fl oz) double cream as directed. Fold in the ground praline.
6 Omit the rum syrup. Spread two-thirds of the hazelnut-praline cream on sponge; roll up and trim as directed.
7 Make the caramel cream sauce (see box, right). Drizzle some sauce on individual plates. Slice the cake and set 2 slices on each plate. Serve with additional sauce.

HOW TO MAKE CARAMEL CREAM SAUCE

A caramel cream sauce has so many uses – spooned over ice cream, with a pie or other pastry.

1 Gently heat 200 g (6 1/2 oz) sugar and 75 ml (2 1/2 fl oz) water in a heavy-based saucepan until the sugar is dissolved. Boil without stirring until the syrup starts to turn golden round the edge. Reduce heat and cook until a deep golden caramel.

ANNE SAYS
'*Let the caramel cook to a deep golden or it will be tasteless, but do not overcook – it burns easily.*'

2 Remove the caramel from the heat and immediately pour in 175 ml (6 fl oz) hot double cream. Whisk at once to mix, then cool.

! TAKE CARE !
The caramel may splutter when the cream is added, so stand at arm's length when pouring.

CHEQUERBOARD CAKE WITH CHOCOLATE GANACHE

🍽 SERVES 8-10 🥣 WORK TIME 50-55 MINUTES* 🍲 BAKING TIME 15-20 MINUTES

EQUIPMENT

scissors

electric mixer

chef's knife

palette knives

rubber spatula

saucepans

wooden spoon

ladle

sieves

whisk

pastry brush

conical sieve

3 x 20-cm (8-inch) round cake tins

3 piping bags

baking parchment

bowls

chopping board

metal skewer

The chequerboard in this tall cake is hidden by a rich chocolate ganache frosting wrapped with a chocolate ribbon. Only when cut is the chequered chocolate and vanilla interior of the cake revealed.
plus cooling and chilling time

INGREDIENTS

plain chocolate

icing sugar

double cream

kirsch

eggs

cocoa powder

vanilla essence

unsalted butter

granulated sugar

raspberry jam

plain flour

baking powder

metric	SHOPPING LIST	imperial
	For the cake	
250 g	unsalted butter + extra for tin	8 oz
375 g	plain flour	12 oz
22.5 ml	baking powder	1 ½ tbsp
45 g	cocoa powder	1 ½ oz
300 g	icing sugar	10 oz
6	eggs	6
10 ml	vanilla essence	2 tsp
125 g	plain chocolate for the ribbon	4 oz
30 ml	cocoa powder for dusting	2 tbsp
	For the kirsch syrup	
125 ml	water	4 fl oz
100 g	granulated sugar	3 ½ oz
30-45 ml	kirsch	2-3 tbsp
	For the raspberry jam glaze	
100 g	raspberry jam	3 ½ oz
30-45 ml	water	2-3 tbsp
	For the chocolate ganache	
250 g	plain chocolate	8 oz
250 ml	double cream	8 fl oz

ORDER OF WORK

1 MAKE THE CAKE MIXTURES

2 PREPARE THE CHEQUERBOARD PATTERN AND BAKE THE CAKE

3 ASSEMBLE THE CHEQUERBOARD

4 DECORATE THE CAKE

1 MAKE THE CAKE MIXTURES

1 Heat the oven to 190°C (375°F, Gas 5). Butter the cake tins and line the bottom of each with baking parchment . Butter the paper.

Baking parchment sticks to melted butter brushed on bottom of tin

Circle of baking parchment has been cut from folded square so it fits exactly inside tin

2 Sift the flour and baking powder and divide equally between 2 medium bowls.

Tap side of sieve to help sugar go through

Icing sugar will cream more easily with butter if it is sifted

3 Sift the cocoa powder into one of the bowls, tapping the side of the sieve to remove any lumps. Beat the butter in a large bowl with the wooden spoon or in the electric mixer until soft and creamy.

4 Sift the icing sugar into the butter and beat in thoroughly.

5 Continue beating the butter and sugar mixture with the wooden spoon or mixer until the mixture is light and fluffy, and doubled in volume, 2-3 minutes.

6 Add the eggs one by one, stirring well after each addition. Add the vanilla essence and stir into the creamed mixture until evenly blended.

ANNE SAYS
'If the mixture begins to separate when adding the eggs, heat the bowl gently over hot water.'

Cake mixtures that are rich in eggs, as this one is, may separate and have curdled appearance

After heating bowl gently over hot water, curdled cake mixture will become creamy again

7 Divide the cake mixture in half and add the cocoa and flour mixture to one portion. Stir well to mix. Stir the plain flour mixture into the other.

2 PREPARE THE CHEQUERBOARD PATTERN AND BAKE THE CAKE

1 Fit 2 of the piping bags with 1.25-cm (½-inch) plain nozzles. Fill 1 bag with cocoa mixture, and the other with white mixture (see box, page 53). Pipe a ring of chocolate mixture against the sides of 2 of the cake tins.

ANNE SAYS
'If your piping bags are small, you may need to fill them in 2 batches.'

Pipe 2 rings of chocolate and 2 of white mixture in each tin, alternating colours, then fill in centre

2 Pipe a ring of white mixture against the side of the third cake tin. Pipe a ring of the white mixture inside the chocolate rings in the first 2 cake tins. Continue alternating rings of chocolate and white mixture until all of the cake tins are full.

3 Bake the layers until the cakes start to shrink from the sides of the tins and the skewer inserted in the centres comes out clean, 15-20 minutes. Meanwhile, make the syrup and glaze (see page 53).

3 ASSEMBLE THE CHEQUERBOARD

1 Make the kirsch syrup: heat the water and sugar in a small pan until the sugar has dissolved. Simmer the syrup 1 minute, remove from heat, cool. Stir in the kirsch.

2 Make the raspberry jam glaze: in another small saucepan, heat the raspberry jam and water, stirring until the jam has melted.

3 Pour the raspberry jam glaze through the conical sieve into a bowl; return the glaze to the saucepan. With scissors, trim a piece of thin card into a round that is slightly smaller than the cake.

HOW TO FILL A PIPING BAG

A variety of nozzles can be used with a piping bag: plain nozzles are suitable for piping cake mixtures and shaping meringue, while fluted nozzles are used for whipped cream decorations.

1 Drop the nozzle into the piping bag. Twist the bag, tucking the bag into the nozzle with your finger.

ANNE SAYS
'*Twisting and tucking keeps filling from leaking out at the bottom.*'

2 Fold the top of the bag over your hand to form a collar and add the mixture to be piped, scraping the rubber spatula against the bag.

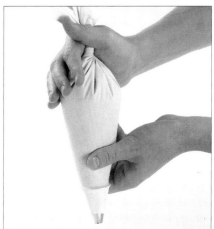

3 When the piping bag is full, unfold the top and twist the top until there is no air left in it.

Moisten cake layers with kirsch syrup

4 Remove the cake layers from the oven. Brush the kirsch syrup on each layer of cake while the layers are still hot.

5 Turn out the cakes on to a wire rack and peel off the parchment.

Melt sieved raspberry jam glaze over low heat before brushing over cake so it will spread easily

6 Brush the base of each layer with the remaining kirsch syrup. Place the card round under one of the cake layers with an outer chocolate ring. Reheat the jam glaze, then brush half of it on the cake layer.

Brush jam glaze evenly all over top of cake and right up to edge

7 Top with the cake that has the outer plain ring and brush it with the remaining jam glaze. Place the remaining cake with the outer chocolate ring on top of the middle layer. Leave the cake to cool while making the ganache.

4 DECORATE THE CAKE

1 Make the chocolate ganache: cut the chocolate into large chunks. Chop them with the chef's knife, or in a food processor using the pulse button. Put the chocolate in a medium bowl. Bring the cream to the boil in a small saucepan and pour it over the chopped chocolate.

2 Whisk the chopped chocolate and cream together until the chocolate has melted completely.

3 Continue beating, with the electric mixer or the whisk, until the ganache is fluffy and cool, 5-10 minutes.

! TAKE CARE !
Do not overbeat the mixture or it will be very stiff and hard to spread.

HOW TO TEMPER MELTED CHOCOLATE

Tempering makes melted chocolate more malleable and shiny. Covering chocolate (couverture) is most often tempered because it has a high cocoa butter content with the greatest gloss. This method is classic, ideal for large amounts of chocolate, while the quicker method, right, is best for smaller amounts.

Make sure work surface is completely dry before pouring melted chocolate on to it

How to temper melted chocolate quickly
Easier than the classic method, left, this can be used for smaller amounts. After melting chocolate, stir gently until it reaches 46°C (115°F) on a sugar thermometer and is very smooth.

Set the bowl of melted chocolate in a bowl of cool (not iced) water. Stir often until it cools to 27°C (80°F), then set in a pan of hot water and heat to 32°C (90°F).

1 Stir melted chocolate gently until it reaches 46°C (115°F) on a sugar thermometer and is very smooth.

2 Pour two-thirds of the chocolate on to a smooth work surface, such as marble or laminate.

3 Work the chocolate by spreading it back and forth with a palette knife for at least 3 minutes until it is thick and on the point of setting (about 27°C/80°F).

4 Using 2 palette knives, quickly transfer the chocolate from the marble to the reserved chocolate in the bowl. Reheat it in the saucepan of hot water, stirring constantly, to 32°C (90°F).

4 Reserve one-third of the ganache frosting for piping on top of the cake. Using a palette knife, spread the side of the cake with some of the remaining ganache frosting.

5 Spread the remainder on top of the cake with the palette knife, then fill in any gaps between the layers – the side should be straight and even.

Warm palette knife first so it will spread frosting smoothly

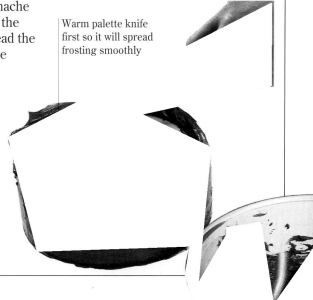

Spread chocolate gently with even pressure

6 Make the chocolate ribbon: cut a 10 x 60-cm (4 x 24-inch) strip from a sheet of baking parchment (it should be the same height as the cake).

7 Chop the chocolate and melt it in a bowl placed in a saucepan half-filled with hot water. For a shiny finish on the chocolate ribbon, temper the melted chocolate (see box, page 55).

8 Ladle the cooled melted or tempered chocolate on to the baking parchment. With a palette knife, quickly spread the chocolate evenly until 1.5 mm ($\frac{1}{16}$ inch) thick.

9 Immediately wrap the chocolate ribbon round the cake, paper-side out.

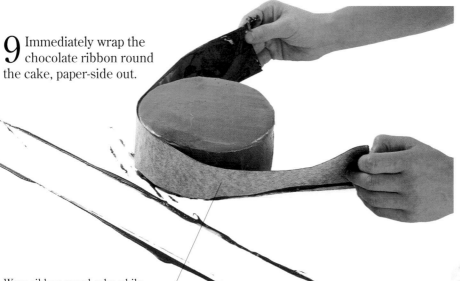

Wrap ribbon round cake while chocolate is still soft; it will then set on to side of cake

10 If the paper overlaps, cut it with scissors.

11 Fit the remaining piping bag with a 1-cm ($\frac{3}{8}$-inch) plain nozzle. Put in the remaining ganache (see box, page 53) and pipe it in 'tear-drop' shapes on top of the cake, starting at the edge and working towards the centre.

ANNE SAYS
'*Slightly overlap tear-drop shapes and pipe in concentric circles to cover top of cake.*'

Pipe ganache in tear-drop shapes

12 Sift the cocoa powder over the top of the cake. Refrigerate until the chocolate ribbon is set, about 1 hour.

If any lumps of cocoa powder are left in bottom of sieve, work them through with your fingertips

13 Carefully peel the baking parchment from the chocolate ribbon round the cake.

🍽 **TO SERVE**
Carefully transfer the cake from its card round to a serving plate. Keep the cake in the refrigerator until serving time.

VARIATION
APRICOT CHEQUERBOARD CAKE

1 Make the cake mixtures and pipe into the prepared round tins as directed.
2 Bake the layers and brush with syrup as directed.
3 Make the glaze with apricot rather than raspberry jam and brush it over the layers.
4 Make the chocolate ganache and frost the cake.
5 Omit the chocolate ribbon and make an apricot sauce: drain 300 g (10 oz) canned apricots in syrup and set aside 4 apricot halves for the decoration; reserve the syrup. Purée the remaining apricots in a food processor or blender, then work through a sieve. Add a little of the reserved syrup to make a sauce of pourable consistency, then stir in 15-30 ml (1-2 tbsp) kirsch if desired.
6 Arrange slices of cake on individual plates; spoon the apricot sauce around. Decorate with apricot slices.

Chequerboard pattern is revealed when cake is sliced

─── **GETTING AHEAD** ───
The cake can be kept in the refrigerator up to 2 days.

Chocolate ribbon is wrapped round cake

CHOCOLATE CREME BRULEE

Crème Brûlée au Chocolat

 SERVES 4   WORK TIME 15-20 MINUTES*   BAKING TIME 10-15 MINUTES

EQUIPMENT

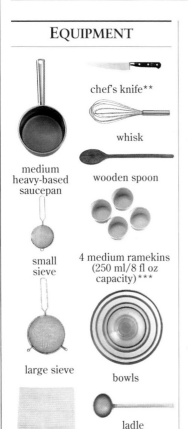

chef's knife**

whisk

medium heavy-based saucepan

wooden spoon

small sieve

4 medium ramekins (250 ml/8 fl oz capacity)***

large sieve

bowls

tea towel

ladle

roasting tin

chopping board

**food processor can also be used
***gratin dishes can also be used

This classic cream is flavoured with dark chocolate, lightly set with egg yolks, and topped with a thin layer of caramelised sugar. You can use ramekins for baking the cream, or gratin dishes if you want the maximum area of crisp caramel topping. Instead of grilling, professional chefs use a blow torch for caramelising the cream without overcooking it. The flame is held over the cream and the sugar is heated until bubbling and brown. Using this method, there is no need to put the cream in the roasting tin with the ice, because the flame is directed only at the sugar and does not heat the cream.

GETTING AHEAD

The chocolate creams can be made up to 8 hours ahead and kept refrigerated. Caramelise the sugar not more than 2 hours before serving.

* plus 1-8 hours chilling time

metric	SHOPPING LIST	imperial
175 g	plain chocolate	6 oz
500 ml	double cream	16 fl oz
4	egg yolks	4
50 g	sugar for sprinkling	1 ³/₄ oz

INGREDIENTS

plain chocolate

double cream

egg yolks

sugar

ANNE SAYS
'*With so few ingredients, the key to a good crème brûlée is that each should be of highest quality. Most important is good-quality chocolate, which makes all the difference. Also important is the cream used – double cream, with a fat content of about 40%, adds richness and smoothness, and should be used rather than whipping or single.*'

ORDER OF WORK

1 MAKE THE CHOCOLATE CREAMS

2 CARAMELISE THE CHOCOLATE CREAMS

HOW TO CHOP CHOCOLATE

Chill chocolate on a warm day before chopping. Chopping board must be dry, because moisture can affect melting.

1 On a chopping board, with a chef's knife, cut chocolate into small chunks.

2 **To chop by hand:** with broad end of knife, chop until chocolate is fine. Rock handle up and down, holding tip down with heel of other hand.

To chop in a food processor: put chocolate chunks into food processor, then chop using the pulse button. If necessary, chop chocolate in several batches.

! TAKE CARE !
Do not overwork the chocolate or the heat of the machine may melt it.

1 MAKE THE CHOCOLATE CREAMS

1 Heat the oven to 200°C (400°F, Gas 6). Chop the chocolate (see box, left). Heat the chocolate with the cream in the saucepan, stirring with the wooden spoon, until melted and smooth. Bring just to the boil. Allow to cool slightly.

Add chopped chocolate to cream and melt in heavy-based pan to prevent mixture burning

Whisk gently so mixture does not become frothy

2 Put the egg yolks in a large bowl and whisk together until just mixed.

3 Pour the chocolate cream slowly into the egg yolks, whisking constantly until evenly mixed.

4 Strain the chocolate cream through the large sieve to remove any bits of cooked egg yolk.

Rest sieve on rim of bowl

Strain chocolate cream to remove any bits of egg

5 Carefully ladle the chocolate cream into the ramekins, dividing it equally between them.

6 Fold the tea towel and put on the bottom of the roasting tin; set the ramekins on the towel. Pour in cold water to come just over halfway up the sides of the dishes.

Towel protects chocolate creams from direct heat of roasting tin and prevents water from bubbling up into them

7 Bake the chocolate creams in the oven until a thin skin forms on top, 10-15 minutes. Remove the ramekins from the roasting tin. Chill the chocolate creams in the refrigerator at least 1 hour or up to 8 hours.

ANNE SAYS
'*The chocolate cream underneath the skin will still be soft.*'

2 CARAMELISE THE CHOCOLATE CREAMS

1 Heat the grill. Sprinkle each chocolate cream evenly with sugar, using the small sieve, to form a thin even layer.

! TAKE CARE !
Wipe off any sugar from the edges of the dishes because it will burn under the grill.

Iced water ensures chocolate cream does not heat under grill

2 Half fill the roasting tin with cold water and ice, and set the ramekins in it. Grill the chocolate creams as close as possible to the heat until the sugar melts and caramelises, 2-3 minutes. Cool a few minutes so the caramel forms a crisp layer.

ANNE SAYS
'*It is essential that the sugar is cooked under very high heat so it caramelises before the cream overcooks.*'

🍴 **TO SERVE**
Place each ramekin on an individual plate. Crack the caramel with the back of a spoon to arrive at the chocolate cream beneath.

Thin, crisp caramel layer is cracked to reveal rich chocolate cream underneath

V A R I A T I O N

CHOCOLATE CREME BRULEE WITH RASPBERRIES

Fresh raspberries are a delicious surprise hidden in the bottom of each chocolate cream.

1 Make the chocolate cream mixture as directed.
2 Sprinkle 6-8 fresh raspberries in the bottom of each of 4 gratin dishes, then fill the dishes with the chocolate cream.
3 Bake the creams and caramelise the sugar as directed.
4 Decorate each cream with a few raspberries just before serving.

CHOCOLATE ORANGE TRUFFLE CAKE

 SERVES 10-12 WORK TIME 35-40 MINUTES* BAKING TIME ABOUT 40 MINUTES

EQUIPMENT

25-cm (10-inch) round cake tin

electric mixer**

chef's knife

small knife

23-cm (9-inch) springform tin

vegetable peeler

kitchen scissors

pastry brush

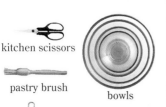

bowls

sieves

cling film

saucepans

wire rack   chopping board

baking parchment

palette knife

rubber spatula

**whisk can also be used

A layer of chocolate sponge cake is crowned with chocolate ganache flavoured with Grand Marnier. Sifted cocoa and a cluster of white chocolate curls complete the ultimate chocolate indulgence. Orange segments steeped in orange juice and Grand Marnier provide the perfect complement.

* plus at least 6 hours chilling time

INGREDIENTS

plain chocolate

white chocolate

flour

eggs

double cream

butter

caster sugar

oranges

Grand Marnier

cocoa powder

metric	SHOPPING LIST	imperial
	For the cake layer	
	butter and flour for tins	
60 g	butter	2 oz
100 g	plain flour	3 ½ oz
30 g	cocoa powder	1 oz
	salt	
4	eggs	4
135 g	caster sugar	4 ½ oz
60-75 ml	Grand Marnier	4-5 tbsp
	For the chocolate ganache	
375 g	plain chocolate	12 oz
375 ml	double cream	12 fl oz
45 ml	Grand Marnier	3 tbsp
	To decorate and finish	
1	bar white chocolate for curls	1
6	oranges	6
45 ml	Grand Marnier	3 tbsp
20 g	cocoa powder	3 tbsp

ORDER OF WORK

1 MAKE THE CAKE LAYER

2 PREPARE THE BASE

3 MAKE THE CHOCOLATE GANACHE

4 PREPARE THE DECORATION AND FINISH THE CAKE

1 MAKE THE CAKE LAYER

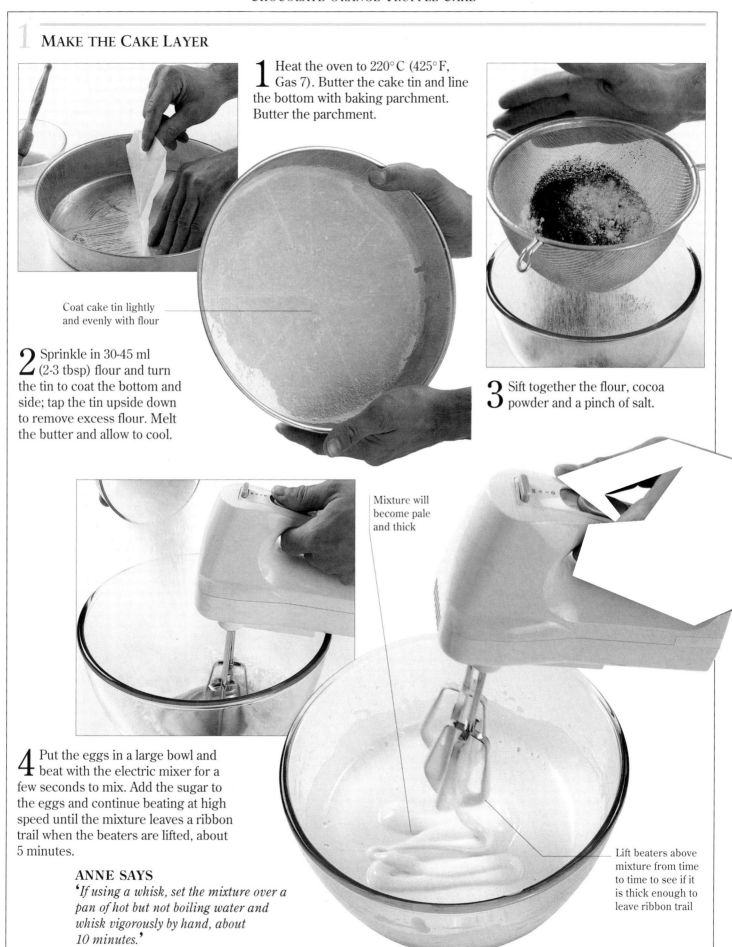

1 Heat the oven to 220°C (425°F, Gas 7). Butter the cake tin and line the bottom with baking parchment. Butter the parchment.

Coat cake tin lightly and evenly with flour

2 Sprinkle in 30-45 ml (2-3 tbsp) flour and turn the tin to coat the bottom and side; tap the tin upside down to remove excess flour. Melt the butter and allow to cool.

3 Sift together the flour, cocoa powder and a pinch of salt.

Mixture will become pale and thick

4 Put the eggs in a large bowl and beat with the electric mixer for a few seconds to mix. Add the sugar to the eggs and continue beating at high speed until the mixture leaves a ribbon trail when the beaters are lifted, about 5 minutes.

Lift beaters above mixture from time to time to see if it is thick enough to leave ribbon trail

ANNE SAYS
'If using a whisk, set the mixture over a pan of hot but not boiling water and whisk vigorously by hand, about 10 minutes.'

5 Sift about one-third of the flour and cocoa mixture over the egg mixture and fold the mixtures together as lightly as possible. Add another third of the flour and cocoa mixture and fold together in the same way.

Fold very lightly with rubber spatula

Turn bowl anti-clockwise as you fold mixtures together

Folded tea towel underneath bowl will keep it steady as you add melted butter

6 Add the remaining flour and cocoa mixture and the cooled, melted butter and fold them in gently but quickly.

7 Pour the mixture into the prepared cake tin, then tap the tin on the work surface to level the mixture and knock out air bubbles.

8 Bake in the heated oven until the cake is risen and just firm to the touch, about 40 minutes. Turn the cake out on to the wire rack. Peel off the paper. Leave the cake to cool.

2 PREPARE THE BASE

1 Trim the cooled cake to fit the springform tin, using the base of the tin as a guide.

Hold small knife vertically and cut cake round base of springform tin with up-and-down sawing action

Side of cake needs to be trimmed so cake will fit in springform tin

2 Lightly butter the bottom and side of the springform tin. Carefully transfer the trimmed cake to the tin. Sprinkle 60-75 ml (4-5 tbsp) Grand Marnier evenly over the top of the cake. Cover and set aside while making the chocolate ganache.

3 MAKE THE CHOCOLATE GANACHE

Hot cream will melt chocolate

1 Cut the chocolate into large chunks. Chop them with the chef's knife or in a food processor. Put the chocolate in a large bowl.

2 Heat the cream until almost boiling, then pour it over the chopped chocolate. Stir until the chocolate has melted. Allow to cool, stirring occasionally.

3 Add the 45 ml (3 tbsp) Grand Marnier to the cream and chocolate mixture and stir until blended.

4 Using the electric mixer, beat the chocolate ganache until fluffy, 5-10 minutes.

! TAKE CARE !
Do not overbeat the mixture or it will be very stiff and hard to spread.

5 With the rubber spatula, or a wooden spoon, turn out the chocolate ganache on top of the cake and smooth the surface. Cover with cling film and chill until firm, at least 6 hours.

4 PREPARE THE DECORATION AND FINISH THE CAKE

1 Using the vegetable peeler, firmly shave curls from the wide side of the bar of white chocolate on to a sheet of baking parchment or a plate.

2 Trim both ends of each orange, set the fruit upright on the chopping board and cut away the peel and all pith, following the curve of the fruit.

3 Working over a bowl, cut down each side of the orange segments to separate them from the membranes. Put the segments in the bowl; sprinkle the Grand Marnier over them.

Cut off peel, working from top to bottom

4 Just before serving, take the cake from the refrigerator. Stand it on top of a bowl, then release the side of the tin to turn out the cake.

5 Mask the centre of the cake with a 7.5-cm (3-inch) round of baking parchment. Sift the cocoa powder on top of the cake and carefully remove the paper round.

Baking parchment round keeps centre of cake plain for white chocolate curls

6 Transfer the cake to a serving plate, using the palette knife, and sprinkle the white chocolate curls over the centre of the cake. Sift a little cocoa powder over the white chocolate curls.

¶❂¶ TO SERVE Slice the cake neatly, then place on individual plates. Arrange orange segments next to the cake and spoon a little of the orange liquid over them.

White chocolate curls are decorative contrast

V A R I A T I O N

CHOCOLATE COFFEE TRUFFLE CAKE

Here coffee-flavoured liqueur replaces the Grand Marnier in Chocolate Orange Truffle Cake.

1 Prepare and bake the chocolate sponge cake, trim the cake to fit the springform tin, and sprinkle over 60-75 ml (4-5 tbsp) Tia Maria or other coffee-flavoured liqueur.
2 Make the ganache, replacing the Grand Marnier with Tia Maria. Spread the ganache over the cake. Chill as directed.
3 Omit the chocolate curls and orange segments and decorate the top of the cake with 90 g (3 oz) chocolate coffee beans, pressing them lightly on to the surface. Sift cocoa powder over the top, then decorate with a few more chocolate coffee beans.

— GETTING AHEAD —
The chocolate sponge cake and ganache can be made and layered 1 day in advance and kept, covered, in the refrigerator. The curls can also be made 1 day in advance. Turn out and decorate the cake 1-2 hours before serving.

CHOCOLATE CHARLOTTE

EQUIPMENT

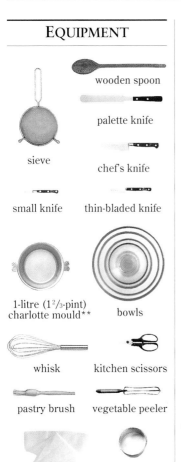

wooden spoon

palette knife

chef's knife

sieve

small knife   thin-bladed knife

1-litre (1²/₃-pint)
charlotte mould**   bowls

whisk   kitchen scissors

pastry brush   vegetable peeler

piping bag and   4-cm (1¹/₂-inch)
medium star nozzle   round pastry
    cutter

saucepans

baking parchment

chopping board
** deep metal bowl can also be
used

*A winter dream come true for chocolate lovers –
half fudge, half cake, baked in a charlotte mould,
then swathed with Chantilly cream and decorated
with chocolate coins and curls. If you don't have
time to make coins, mint sprigs or crystallised
violets make attractive alternatives.*

GETTING AHEAD

The charlotte can be prepared up to 1 week ahead and kept
in the refrigerator, or it can be frozen. The chocolate coins
can be layered with baking parchment and stored in the
refrigerator up to 1 week. Make the Chantilly cream and
decorate the charlotte not more than 2 hours before serving.

* plus 24 hours chilling time

metric	SHOPPING LIST	imperial
125 g	plain chocolate for coins	4 oz
1	bar plain chocolate for curls	1
	For the chocolate charlotte	
	butter for mould	
250 g	plain chocolate	8 oz
175 ml	strong black coffee	6 fl oz
250 g	unsalted butter	8 oz
200 g	caster sugar	6¹/₂ oz
4	eggs	4
	For the Chantilly cream	
375 ml	double cream	12 fl oz
22.5 ml	caster sugar	1¹/₂ tbsp
3.75 ml	vanilla essence	³/₄ tsp

INGREDIENTS

plain chocolate

unsalted butter

double cream

eggs

strong black
coffee

vanilla essence

caster sugar

chocolate bar

ORDER OF WORK

1 MAKE THE
CHOCOLATE
CHARLOTTE

2 TURN OUT THE
CHARLOTTE

3 DECORATE THE
CHARLOTTE

1 MAKE THE CHOCOLATE CHARLOTTE

1 Brush the inside of the mould with melted butter. Line the bottom with parchment and butter the paper. Chill while preparing the mixture. Heat the oven to 180°C (350°F, Gas 4).

2 Cut the chocolate into large chunks. Chop them with the chef's knife, or in a food processor using the pulse button. Put the chocolate into a heavy-based medium saucepan, add the coffee and heat, stirring with the wooden spoon, until the mixture is smooth and thick but still falls easily from the spoon, 5-7 minutes.

Sugar is added to butter and melted chocolate mixture

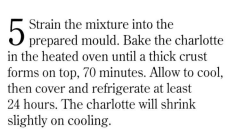

As soon as chocolate mixture comes to the boil, remove from heat

3 Cut the butter into pieces and add to the saucepan followed by the sugar. Heat, stirring, until the butter has melted and the sugar dissolved. Bring the mixture almost to the boil, stirring well with the wooden spoon.

4 Remove the saucepan from the heat and whisk in the eggs, one by one, whisking well after each addition.

ANNE SAYS
'The eggs will cook and thicken in the heat of the mixture.'

5 Strain the mixture into the prepared mould. Bake the charlotte in the heated oven until a thick crust forms on top, 70 minutes. Allow to cool, then cover and refrigerate at least 24 hours. The charlotte will shrink slightly on cooling.

ANNE SAYS
'Under the crust, the mixture will still be quite soft.'

2 TURN OUT THE CHARLOTTE

1 Run the thin-bladed knife between the charlotte and the mould to loosen it from the mould.

2 Dip the base of the mould briefly into a pan of warm water, then lift it out and dry the mould.

3 Hold a serving plate over the mould, invert, then lift off the mould. Peel off the paper. Chill the charlotte until ready to decorate.

HOW TO MAKE CHOCOLATE COINS

Chocolate can be shaped into geometric decorations. Once set, they can be layered with baking parchment and stored in the refrigerator up to 1 week.

2 With a 4-cm (1 ½-inch) pastry cutter or the broad end of a piping nozzle, cut circles in the chocolate. Allow to set.

! TAKE CARE !
Do not refrigerate the coins before they are set because the chocolate will shrink away from the paper and buckle.

1 Cut a strip of baking parchment 30 cm (12 inches) long and 5 cm (2 inches) wide. Cut the chocolate into large chunks. Chop them with a chef's knife, or in a food processor using the pulse button. Melt the chocolate in a bowl set in a saucepan half-filled with hot water, then cool slightly. Spread the chocolate on the paper in an even layer about 1.5 mm (¹⁄₁₆ inch) thick. Leave to cool until on the point of setting.

ANNE SAYS
'*For a shiny finish on the chocolate coins, temper the chocolate after melting it - see box, page 55.*'

3 When the chocolate is firm, flip the paper strip over on to a sheet of parchment. Loosen the end of the strip with the tip of a small knife, then peel away paper. Remove the coins.

Use tip of small knife to lift chocolate coins

3 DECORATE THE CHARLOTTE

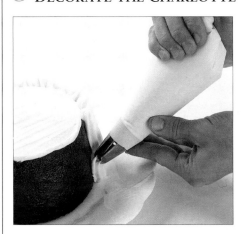

1 Use the 125 g (4 oz) plain chocolate to make 8 chocolate coins (see box, page 70). Make the Chantilly cream: pour the cream into a chilled bowl and whip until soft peaks form. Add the sugar and vanilla essence and continue whipping until stiff peaks form. Spread a little of the cream over the top of the charlotte using the palette knife. Put the remaining cream into the piping bag and pipe vertical lines to cover the side of the charlotte.

2 Pipe swirls of Chantilly cream round the base and top edge of the charlotte.

Squeeze piping bag gently and evenly to pipe

3 With the vegetable peeler, make curls from the bar of plain chocolate. Sprinkle over the top. Arrange the chocolate coins round the base of the charlotte.

VARIATION

SMALL CHOCOLATE CHARLOTTES

These individual servings of Chocolate Charlotte are a fine finish for a winter dinner party.

1 Prepare the chocolate charlotte mixture as directed.
2 Butter the inside of 8 ramekins (175 ml/6 fl oz capacity); line the bottoms with foil. Fill the ramekins with the charlotte mixture.
3 Bake until crusty, 45 minutes, a little longer if necessary. Allow to cool, then refrigerate and turn out as directed.
4 Pipe stars of Chantilly cream all over the charlottes, using a small star nozzle, and decorate with chocolate coins, making double the number in the main recipe.

Fudgy chocolate charlotte is covered with piped Chantilly cream

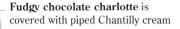

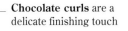

Chocolate curls are a delicate finishing touch

CHOCOLATE MOUSSE WITH HAZELNUTS AND WHISKY

♥◎♥ SERVES 6 ⚬ WORK TIME 20-25 MINUTES ❄ CHILLING TIME 1-1½ HOURS

EQUIPMENT

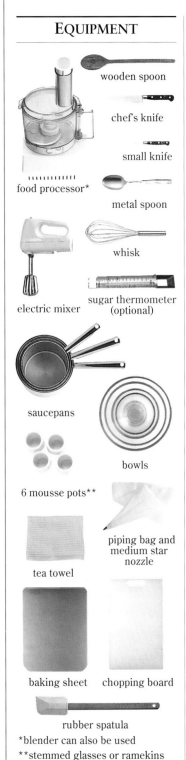

wooden spoon

chef's knife

small knife

food processor*

metal spoon

whisk

electric mixer

sugar thermometer (optional)

saucepans

bowls

6 mousse pots**

tea towel

piping bag and medium star nozzle

baking sheet   chopping board

rubber spatula

*blender can also be used

**stemmed glasses or ramekins can also be used

Toasted hazelnuts create texture, and whisky gives zip, to this version of classic dark chocolate mousse. If you prefer, you can substitute almost any spirit or liqueur for the whisky – rum, brandy or Grand Marnier taste particularly good with the flavour of chocolate.

GETTING AHEAD

The mousse can be made 1 day ahead and kept, covered, in the refrigerator. Decorate just before serving.

metric	SHOPPING LIST	imperial
60 g	hazelnuts	2 oz
250 g	plain chocolate	8 oz
125 ml	water	4 fl oz
15 ml	unsalted butter	1 tbsp
3	eggs	3
30 ml	whisky	2 tbsp
50 g	caster sugar	1¾ oz
	For the Chantilly cream	
125 ml	double cream	4 fl oz
15 ml	caster sugar	1 tbsp
10 ml	whisky	2 tsp

INGREDIENTS

hazelnuts

plain chocolate

unsalted butter

eggs

double cream

whisky

caster sugar

ANNE SAYS

'*Cold mousse, with a frothy texture, is one of the most popular French desserts. Some mousses need gelatine to hold them; chocolate sets by itself. For a light mousse, the chocolate mixture and Italian meringue should be about the same consistency when they are folded together.*'

ORDER OF WORK

1 MAKE THE MOUSSE MIXTURE

2 DECORATE THE MOUSSE

1 MAKE THE MOUSSE MIXTURE

1 Toast and skin the hazelnuts (see box, below). Grind them in the food processor, reserving 6 whole nuts for decoration. Alternatively, use a rotary grater.

! TAKE CARE !

Do not overwork or the oil will be released from the nuts, creating a paste.

Process hazelnuts all at same time so they will be evenly ground

2 Cut the chocolate into large chunks. Chop them with the chef's knife, or in a food processor using the pulse button, then place in a medium heavy-based saucepan and add half of the water. Heat gently, stirring, until melted and the consistency of double cream, 3-5 minutes.

3 Remove the saucepan of melted chocolate from the heat and stir in the butter, cut in pieces.

4 Separate the eggs. Whisk the egg yolks into the chocolate mixture one by one, whisking well after each addition. Whisk the chocolate mixture over low heat about 4 minutes to ensure that the yolks are cooked.

HOW TO TOAST AND SKIN NUTS

Toasting nuts intensifies their flavour and adds crunch to their texture. It also loosens thin skin from nuts such as hazelnuts, so the skins can be removed easily by rubbing with a rough tea towel.

1 Heat the oven to 180°C (350°F, Gas 4). Spread the nuts on a baking sheet and bake until lightly browned, stirring occasionally.

! TAKE CARE !
Watch so the nuts do not burn or they will have a very bitter flavour.

2 To remove skins from hazelnuts, transfer the nuts from the baking sheet to a rough tea towel and rub while still hot.

5 Remove from the heat and whisk in the hazelnuts and whisky. Allow the mixture to cool to tepid.

HOW TO WHISK EGG WHITES UNTIL STIFF

Egg whites should be whisked until stiff but not dry. For egg whites to whisk properly, the whites, bowl and whisk must be completely free from any trace of water, grease or egg yolk. A copper bowl and a large balloon whisk are the classic French utensils used for whisking egg whites. A metal or glass bowl with a balloon whisk or electric mixer can also be used.

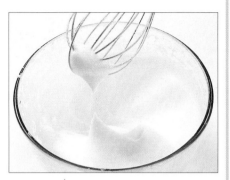

1 Begin whisking the whites slowly. When they are foamy and white, increase the whisking speed. If you like, add a small pinch of salt or cream of tartar to help achieve maximum volume.

! TAKE CARE !
Do not stop or slow down the whisking at this stage or the egg whites may 'turn', becoming grainy and hard to fold into other ingredients.

2 The whites are whisked enough when they form a stiff peak when the whisk is lifted, gathering in the whisk wires and sticking without falling. The whites should be used at once because they separate quickly on standing.

! TAKE CARE !
Do not overbeat the egg whites; if they are overbeaten, the correct texture cannot be reconstituted.

Use small, deep saucepan for boiling sugar syrup

6 Meanwhile, put remaining water in a small pan, add the sugar and heat until dissolved, stirring occasionally. Boil without stirring until syrup is 120°C (248°F) on thermometer.

ANNE SAYS
'*To test the syrup without using a thermometer, take the pan from the heat, dip a teaspoon in the hot syrup and remove it. Allow the syrup to cool a few seconds, then take a little between your finger and thumb: it should form a firm, pliable ball.*'

Hold saucepan firmly so stream of sugar syrup can be controlled

7 Whisk the egg whites until stiff (see box, above). Gradually pour in the hot sugar syrup, whisking constantly. Continue whisking until the meringue is cool and stiff, about 5 minutes.

ANNE SAYS
'*To steady the bowl as you whisk, set it on a folded dampened tea towel.*'

8 Stir one-quarter of the meringue into the tepid chocolate mixture.

9 Add the meringue and chocolate mixture to the remaining meringue and fold in gently.

Divide mousse mixture equally among pots

10 Spoon the chocolate mousse into the mousse pots and chill until set, at least 1 hour.

2 DECORATE THE MOUSSE

1 Make the Chantilly cream: pour the cream into a chilled bowl and whip until soft peaks form. Add the sugar and whisky and continue whipping until stiff peaks form. Fill the piping bag and star nozzle with the cream and decorate the top of each mousse with a single large rosette and a whole hazelnut.

ANNE SAYS
'*If you prefer, chop the reserved hazelnuts and sprinkle over the cream.*'

Rosette of whipped cream, sweetened and flavoured with whisky

VARIATION

DOUBLE-CHOCOLATE MOUSSE

Chunks of white chocolate provide a colour contrast in this variation.

1 Omit the hazelnuts and whisky.
2 Coarsely chop 60 g (2 oz) white chocolate or use 60 g (2 oz) white chocolate chips.
3 Make the mousse as directed, and fold in three-quarters of the white chocolate before chilling.
4 Omit the Chantilly cream and sprinkle the mousse with the remaining white chocolate before serving.

CHOCOLATE SOUFFLE

EQUIPMENT

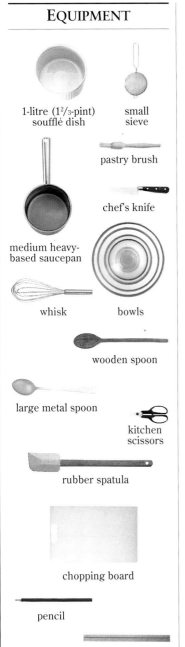

1-litre (1²/₃-pint) soufflé dish

small sieve

pastry brush

chef's knife

medium heavy-based saucepan

whisk

bowls

wooden spoon

large metal spoon

kitchen scissors

rubber spatula

chopping board

pencil

ruler

thin card

My favourite soufflé: the chocolate is so thick and rich that it holds the whisked egg whites without any added flour. Be careful not to overcook the soufflé – the best part is the soft, creamy centre that forms a sauce for the crisp outside. To serve a soufflé correctly, use 2 large metal spoons. Plunge them into the centre of the soufflé and scoop out a wedge so each serving is partly firm, partly soft.

GETTING AHEAD

You can prepare the chocolate mixture for the soufflé up to the end of step 5 up to 3 hours before baking. Keep it, covered, in the refrigerator. Whisk the egg whites and fold them into the chocolate mixture just before baking.

metric	SHOPPING LIST	imperial
	butter for dish	
125 g	plain chocolate	4 oz
125 ml	double cream	4 fl oz
3	eggs	3
30 ml	brandy	2 tbsp
2.5 ml	vanilla essence	½ tsp
2	egg whites	2
45 ml	caster sugar	3 tbsp
	For sprinkling	
30-45 ml	icing sugar	2-3 tbsp

INGREDIENTS

eggs

plain chocolate

double cream

brandy

icing sugar

egg whites

vanilla essence

caster sugar

ANNE SAYS
'When baking a soufflé, set the dish low down in the oven so the soufflé has room to rise. If you open the oven door during baking to turn the dish so that it cooks evenly, the soufflé will not sink, but do avoid drafts.'

ORDER OF WORK

1 PREPARE THE CHOCOLATE MIXTURE

2 BAKE THE CHOCOLATE SOUFFLE

1 PREPARE THE CHOCOLATE MIXTURE

1 Brush the soufflé dish with melted butter. Heat the oven to 220°C (425°F, Gas 7).

2 Cut the chocolate into large chunks. Chop them with the chef's knife, or in a food processor using the pulse button. Put the chocolate in the saucepan, add the cream, stir to mix, then heat gently, stirring, until melted and smooth, about 5 minutes.

Pour cream over chopped chocolate and stir to mix before placing over heat

3 If the mixture is a little thin, simmer it to the consistency of double cream. Remove the pan from the heat.

Check consistency of chocolate and cream mixture by lifting spoonful out of pan

5 Remove from the heat and whisk in the brandy and vanilla essence.

4 Separate the eggs. Whisk the egg yolks into the hot mixture one by one, stirring well with the whisk after each addition. Whisk the chocolate mixture over low heat about 4 minutes to ensure that the egg yolks are cooked.

Whisk in each egg yolk before adding next one so mixture stays smooth

6 If necessary, reheat the chocolate mixture until hot to the touch. Whisk the 5 egg whites until stiff. Sprinkle in the sugar and continue whisking until glossy to form a light meringue, about 20 seconds. Cut and fold the meringue and chocolate mixtures together (see box, page 78).

HOW TO CUT AND FOLD 2 MIXTURES TOGETHER

Two mixtures can be folded together most easily if their consistency is similar. If one ingredient is much lighter or more liquid than the other, such as the light meringue and heavier chocolate and cream mixture in this soufflé, first stir a little of the lighter mixture into the heavier one to soften it.

1 Spoon one-quarter of the light mixture over the heavier mixture and stir in with a rubber spatula.

2 Add this mixture to the remaining meringue in the bowl.

Scoop under contents of bowl and bring spatula up, turning bowl anti-clockwise

Take spatula down into mixture, continuing to turn bowl anti-clockwise

Cut down into centre of mixture with edge of spatula

3 With a rubber spatula, or a wooden or metal spoon, cut down into the centre of the bowl, scoop under the contents and turn them over in a rolling motion. At the same time, turn the bowl anti-clockwise.

ANNE SAYS
'*This should be a synchronised movement: cut and scoop with the spatula in one hand, turn the bowl with the other. Using this method, the spatula reaches the maximum volume of mixture in one movement, so mixture is folded quickly and loses a minimum of air.*'

Bring spatula round under mixture again, turning bowl anti-clockwise

2 BAKE THE CHOCOLATE SOUFFLE

1 Gently pour the soufflé mixture into the prepared dish.

2 Carefully place the soufflé in the heated oven and bake until puffed, 15-18 minutes.

🍴 **TO SERVE** Make a template out of thin card. Remove the soufflé from the oven and quickly place the template on top. Sprinkle with icing sugar, using the sieve, then carefully remove the template. Serve immediately.

— Place soufflé on serving plate for easy handling

V A R I A T I O N

INDIVIDUAL CHOCOLATE SOUFFLES

The chocolate soufflé mixture bakes well as individual servings.

1 Butter 4 large ramekins (250 ml/ 8 fl oz) capacity).
2 Prepare the chocolate mixture as directed in the main recipe.
3 Divide the mixture among the ramekins and bake 10-12 minutes.
4 Sprinkle with cocoa powder and icing sugar and serve immediately, with crisp biscuits, if you like.

V A R I A T I O N

AMARETTO CHOCOLATE SOUFFLE

Italian Amaretti biscuits soaked in Amaretto liqueur are a delicious surprise in this soufflé.

1 Put 3-4 Amaretti biscuits in a plastic bag and crush them with a rolling pin. Reserve for decoration.

2 Lay 14-16 more Amaretti biscuits upside down in a shallow dish and brush generously with 60 ml (2 fl oz) Amaretto liqueur.
3 Butter a 1.2-litre (2-pint) soufflé dish.
4 Prepare the chocolate mixture as directed, replacing the brandy with Amaretto liqueur.
5 Pour half of the mixture into the prepared dish, then lay the soaked biscuits on top. Cover with the remaining soufflé mixture.
6 Bake the soufflé as directed in the main recipe.
7 Sprinkle with the crushed biscuits and serve at once.

STEAMED MEXICAN CHOCOLATE PUDDING WITH APRICOT SAUCE

🍽 SERVES 6-8 🥄 WORK TIME 20-25 MINUTES 🍲 STEAMING TIME 60-70 MINUTES

EQUIPMENT

bowl sieve

conical sieve

chef's knife

kitchen scissors

metal skewer

wooden spoon

ladle

deep 1-litre (1²/₃-pint) pudding basin

whisk

electric mixer

baking parchment

large pan with lid*

tea towel

saucepans

pastry brush

bowls

food processor**

rubber spatula

*steamer can also be used

**blender can also be used

Christmas plum pudding is only the beginning of steamed pudding possibilities. The flavour of this steamed chocolate pudding is accentuated, Mexican-style, with cinnamon, while the apricot sauce and garnish provide bright colour.

GETTING AHEAD

The pudding and apricot sauce can be made up to 3 days ahead and refrigerated. Keep the pudding in the basin and reheat it by steaming 30-40 minutes. Warm the sauce just before serving.

INGREDIENTS

chocolate cake

plain chocolate

canned apricots

vanilla essence

caster sugar

unsalted butter

milk

eggs

kirsch

ground cinnamon

ground cloves

metric	SHOPPING LIST	imperial
	For the pudding mixture	
175 g	chocolate cake	6 oz
15 ml	ground cinnamon	1 tbsp
5 ml	ground cloves	1 tsp
90 g	plain chocolate	3 oz
175 ml	milk	6 fl oz
	butter for pudding bowl	
60 g	unsalted butter	2 oz
50 g	caster sugar	1³/₄ oz
2	eggs	2
2.5 ml	vanilla essence	¹/₂ tsp
	For the apricot sauce	
300 g	canned apricots in syrup	10 oz
15-30 ml	kirsch (optional)	1-2 tbsp

ORDER OF WORK

1 PREPARE THE PUDDING MIXTURE

2 STEAM THE PUDDING

3 MAKE THE APRICOT SAUCE

1 PREPARE THE PUDDING MIXTURE

1 Cut the cake into pieces and work, a few pieces at a time, in the food processor to make crumbs. Add spices.

2 Cut the chocolate into large chunks. Chop them with the chef's knife, or in a food processor using the pulse button. Heat the chocolate with the milk in a heavy-based medium saucepan, stirring until melted and smooth. Bring the mixture to the boil and remove from the heat.

Shake food processor bowl and tap gently on edge of saucepan to release cake crumbs

3 Add the spiced cake crumbs to the chocolate milk mixture. Stir well with the wooden spoon, then leave until absorbed, 20-30 minutes.

4 Brush the pudding basin evenly with melted butter.

5 Using the electric mixer, cream the butter in a large bowl. Add the sugar and beat until fluffy and light, 2-3 minutes.

ANNE SAYS
'*You can also cream the butter and sugar with a wooden spoon.*'

Add sugar to creamed butter while beating with electric mixer

6 Separate the eggs. Add the egg yolks to the butter mixture one by one, beating well after each addition.

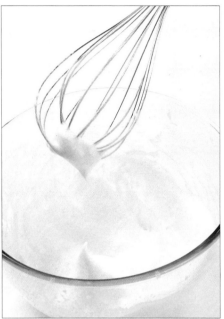

7 Stir the chocolate cake crumbs and vanilla essence into the creamed mixture until evenly blended.

8 Whisk the egg whites until stiff, then fold them into the chocolate pudding mixture.

9 Pour the mixture into the prepared pudding basin, scraping it all in with the rubber spatula.

2 STEAM THE PUDDING

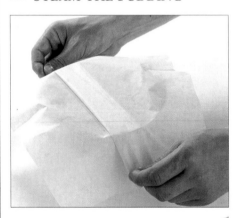

1 Pour enough water into the large pan to come about halfway up the side of the pudding basin. Put a rack or upturned saucer on the bottom of the pan. Bring the water to the boil. Butter a sheet of baking parchment, pleat it in the centre, and lay it over the basin.

2 Lay the tea towel, also pleated in the centre, on the paper and tie it securely under the lip of the basin with kitchen string.

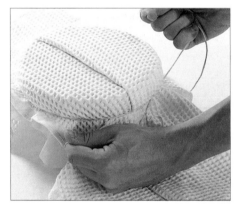

3 Knot the ends of the towel together. Trim off the excess baking parchment. Lift the basin by the knotted towel, and lower it into the pan.

'Handle' made from knotted tea towel is convenient for lifting bowl in and out of pan

ANNE SAYS
'*If the pudding is not done, wrap a piece of foil tightly over the basin and continue cooking.*'

Insert skewer to test whether pudding is cooked

4 Steam the pudding 60-70 minutes. Lift the pudding out of the pan. Cut the string and remove the tea towel and paper. The pudding is done if the skewer inserted in the centre is hot to the touch when withdrawn after 30 seconds.

3 MAKE THE APRICOT SAUCE

Tip drained apricots straight from sieve into food processor bowl

1 Drain the apricots, reserving the syrup. Set aside 3 apricot halves and purée the remainder in the food processor.

2 Work the purée through the conical sieve into a saucepan, pressing with the ladle. Add a little of the reserved syrup to make a pourable sauce, then stir in the kirsch if you like. Gently warm the sauce.

¡◎! TO SERVE
Turn out the pudding on to a serving dish and spoon some of the warm apricot sauce round. Arrange the reserved apricot halves on top of the pudding. Serve any remaining apricot sauce separately.

Apricots add colour and make attractive flower pattern on top of pudding

---

V A R I A T I O N
STEAMED MEXICAN CHOCOLATE PUDDING WITH CHOCOLATE SAUCE

A rich, dark chocolate sauce takes the place of the apricot sauce in the main recipe for chocolate pudding.

1 Prepare and steam the pudding as directed.
2 Meanwhile, make the chocolate sauce: chop 175 g (6 oz) plain chocolate and heat it with 75 ml (2 ½ fl oz) water and 30 ml (2 tbsp) sugar in a small saucepan over low heat, stirring until the chocolate is melted and the sugar has dissolved. Bring to the boil and cook, stirring, until thickened, 1-2 minutes.
3 Turn out the pudding on to a serving dish and serve with the chocolate sauce.

Warm apricot sauce is perfect complement for hot steamed pudding spiced with cinnamon and cloves

CHOCOLATE AND PEAR TARTLETS

Tartelettes Tante Katherine

 MAKES 8 TARTLETS   WORK TIME 30-35 MINUTES*   BAKING TIME 25-30 MINUTES

EQUIPMENT

food processor**

sieve

small knife

chef's knife

eight tartlet tins

ladle

vegetable peeler

pastry brush

bowls

conical sieve

melon baller

baking sheet

cling film

chopping board

whisk

greaseproof paper

palette knife***

rolling pin

** blender can also be used

***pastry scraper can also be used

INGREDIENTS

pears

plain chocolate

flour

eggs

single cream

vanilla essence

kirsch

unsalted butter

caster sugar

egg yolks

raspberries

icing sugar

No wonder Katherine was the favourite aunt of our neighbours in Normandy. These tartlets are superbly flavoured.

* plus about 30 minutes chilling time

metric	SHOPPING LIST	imperial
150 g	plain chocolate	5 oz
2	large, ripe pears, total weight 750 g (1½ lb)	2
15-30 ml	caster sugar for sprinkling	1-2 tbsp
	mint sprigs for decoration	
	For the pastry dough	
175 g	plain flour	6 oz
90 g	unsalted butter + extra for tins	3 oz
60 g	caster sugar	2 oz
2.5 ml	salt	½ tsp
2.5 ml	vanilla essence	½ tsp
3	egg yolks	3
	For the custard	
1	egg	1
125 ml	single cream	4 fl oz
15 ml	kirsch	1 tbsp
	For the raspberry coulis	
500 g	raspberries	1 lb
15-30 ml	kirsch (optional)	1-2 tbsp
30-45 ml	icing sugar	2-3 tbsp

ORDER OF WORK

1 MAKE THE PASTRY DOUGH

2 LINE THE TARTLET TINS

3 FILL AND BAKE THE TARTLETS; MAKE THE COULIS

1 MAKE THE PASTRY DOUGH

1 Sift the flour on to a work surface, tapping the side of the strainer.

Sift flour to aerate it and make pastry light

Use fine-meshed sieve to remove any lumps from flour and tap with your hand on side to help flour sift through

2 Put the butter between 2 sheets of greaseproof paper and pound with the rolling pin to soften it slightly.

3 Make a well in the centre of the flour with your hand.

4 Put the sugar, salt and vanilla essence in the well.

5 Add the butter to the ingredients in the well. With your fingertips, work the ingredients in the well until thoroughly mixed.

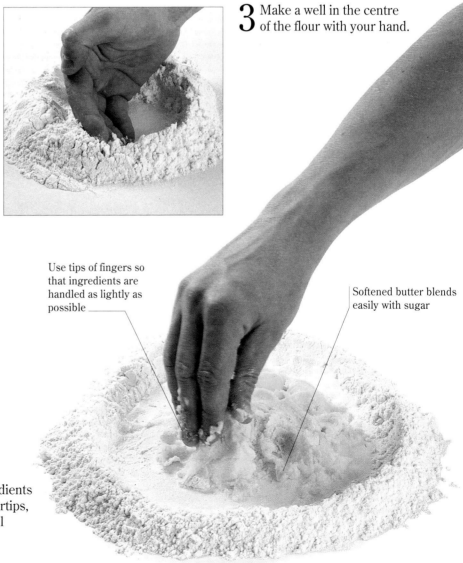

Use tips of fingers so that ingredients are handled as lightly as possible

Softened butter blends easily with sugar

6 Add the egg yolks and work into the ingredients in the well. Draw in the flour with the palette knife. With your fingers, work the flour into the other ingredients until coarse crumbs form. Press the dough into a ball.

Draw ingredients together with fingertips

Push flour into well little by little

7 Sprinkle the work surface lightly with flour, then blend the dough by pushing the ball away from you with the heel of your hand.

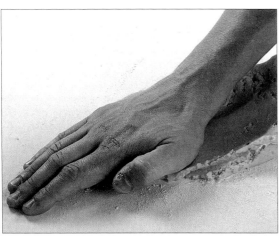

Use palette knife to scrape up dough from work surface

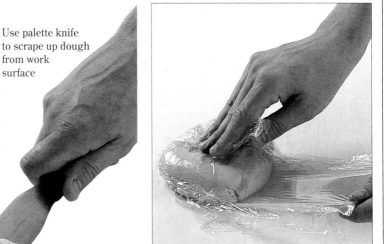

8 Gather up the dough and continue to blend until it is very smooth and peels away from the work surface in one piece, 1-2 minutes.

9 Shape the dough into a ball again, wrap in cling film, and chill until firm, about 30 minutes.

! TAKE CARE !
Pastry doughs made with a lot of sugar are particularly delicate. Be sure to chill the dough before rolling out.

2 LINE THE TARTLET TINS

1 Brush the insides of eight 10-cm (4-inch) tartlet tins with melted butter. Group 4 of the tartlet tins together, with their edges nearly touching.

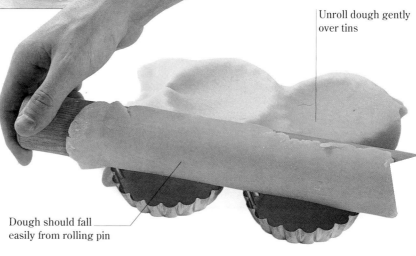

Unroll dough gently over tins

Dough should fall easily from rolling pin

2 Sprinkle the work surface lightly with flour. Divide the ball of dough in half and roll it out to 3 mm (⅛ inch) thickness. Roll the dough loosely round the rolling pin and drape it over the 4 tins to cover them completely.

3 Tear off a small piece of dough from the edge, form it into a ball, dip it in flour, and use it to push the dough into the tins.

4 Roll the rolling pin over the tops of the tins to cut off excess dough.

ANNE SAYS
'Excess dough can be rolled out again and then used to line any remaining tartlet tins.'

5 With your fingers, press the dough into the flutes of each tin to form a deep shell. Repeat with the 4 remaining tins and dough.

3 FILL AND BAKE THE TARTLETS; MAKE THE COULIS

1 Heat the oven to 200°C (400°F, Gas 6). Heat the baking sheet. Cut the chocolate into large chunks. Finely chop them with the chef's knife, or in a food processor using the pulse button. Sprinkle into each tartlet shell.

Scatter finely chopped chocolate evenly in tartlet shells

2 To make the custard, whisk the egg, cream and kirsch together until thoroughly mixed.

3 Spoon 30-45 ml (2-3 tbsp) of the kirsch custard over the chopped chocolate in each tartlet shell.

4 Peel the pears, cut them in half, and remove the cores with the melon baller. Cut out the stalk end with the small knife.

ANNE SAYS
'*To keep the pears from turning brown, sprinkle them with a little lemon juice.*'

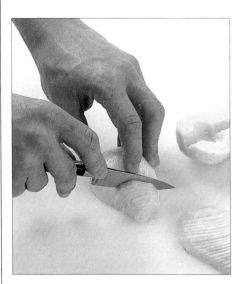

Lay pear slices in tartlet shells to resemble flower shape

5 With the small knife, cut each pear half crosswise into very thin slices.

6 Arrange the pear slices in a flower-petal design on the custard so that the slices overlap.

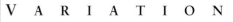

7 Press the pear slices down lightly into the custard, then sprinkle the pears evenly with the sugar.

8 Place the tartlet tins on the heated baking sheet near the bottom of the heated oven. Bake 10 minutes, then reduce the heat to 180°C (350°F, Gas 4) and continue baking the tartlets until the pastry is golden and the custard is set, 15-20 minutes longer.

ANNE SAYS
'Putting the tartlet tins on a heated baking sheet ensures that the bases of the tartlet shells cook thoroughly.'

9 Meanwhile, make the raspberry coulis: pick over the berries, then purée them in the food processor. Add the kirsch, if using, then icing sugar to taste and purée again. Sieve to remove the seeds.

VARIATION

CHOCOLATE AND APPLE TARTLETS

Apples replace pears in these tartlets, with the added spice of cinnamon.

1 Prepare the pastry dough and line the tartlet tins as directed in the recipe for Chocolate and Pear Tartlets.
2 Peel and core 3 apples, total weight about 500 g (1 lb). Cut them into small chunks.
3 Heat about 30 ml (2 tbsp) unsalted butter in a large saucepan. Add the apple chunks and sprinkle them with 15-30 ml (1-2 tbsp) sugar and 10 ml (2 tsp) ground cinnamon. Sauté briskly until slightly softened and caramelised, stirring occasionally, 3-5 minutes.
4 Sprinkle the chopped chocolate into the tartlet shells and spoon the custard over the top.
5 Spread the apples on the custard, pressing them down lightly. Bake as directed.

—**GETTING AHEAD**—
The pastry dough can be made up to 2 days in advance and kept in the refrigerator, or it can be frozen. The tartlets can be kept 6-8 hours, but are best eaten the day they are baked.

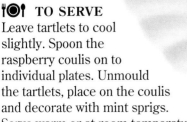

TO SERVE
Leave tartlets to cool slightly. Spoon the raspberry coulis on to individual plates. Unmould the tartlets, place on the coulis and decorate with mint sprigs. Serve warm or at room temperature.

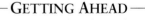

Mint sprig is an appealing decoration

PROFITEROLES WITH CHOCOLATE ICE CREAM

¶O¶ SERVES 8 ⌣ WORK TIME 25-30 MINUTES* ☶ BAKING TIME 25-30 MINUTES

EQUIPMENT

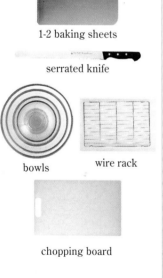

saucepans

sieve

piping bag with plain nozzle

small sharp knife

pastry brush

melon baller**

chef's knife

fork

wooden spoons

1-2 baking sheets

serrated knife

bowls

wire rack

chopping board

**small ice-cream scoop or
2 teaspoons can also be used

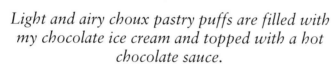

Light and airy choux pastry puffs are filled with my chocolate ice cream and topped with a hot chocolate sauce.

GETTING AHEAD

All the elements can be prepared ahead: the ice cream and sauce can be frozen up to 2 weeks, and the choux puffs can be kept in an airtight container 2-3 days. Assemble the profiteroles just before serving.

* plus time to make ice cream

metric	SHOPPING LIST	imperial
³/₄ quantity	Chocolate Ice Cream (see page 106)	³/₄ quantity
	For the choux pastry	
	butter for baking sheet	
100 g	plain flour	3 ¹/₂ oz
75 g	unsalted butter	2 ¹/₂ oz
175 ml	water	6 fl oz
2.5 ml	salt	¹/₂ tsp
3-4	eggs	3-4
	For the egg glaze	
1	egg	1
2.5 ml	salt	¹/₂ tsp
	For the chocolate sauce	
375 g	plain chocolate	12 oz
250 ml	double cream	8 fl oz
30 ml	Cognac (optional)	2 tbsp

INGREDIENTS

plain chocolate

eggs

double cream

unsalted butter

plain flour

Cognac

chocolate ice cream

ORDER OF WORK

1 **PREPARE THE CHOUX PASTRY**

2 **MAKE THE GLAZE; BAKE THE PUFFS**

3 **MAKE THE CHOCOLATE SAUCE AND FINISH THE PROFITEROLES**

1 PREPARE THE CHOUX PASTRY

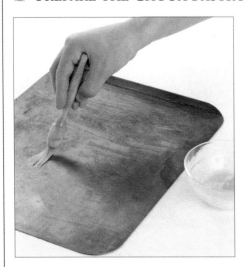

1 Heat the oven to 200°C (400°F, Gas 6). Brush the baking sheet evenly with melted butter. Sift the flour into a medium-sized bowl.

2 Cut the butter into pieces. Put them into a large saucepan with the water and salt.

Combine water and butter off the stove so they melt and blend together when heated

3 Heat until the butter has melted. Bring the mixture just to the boil. Remove from heat.

! TAKE CARE !
The water should not boil before the butter melts or the evaporation will affect the dough proportions.

4 Add the flour to the butter mixture all at once and beat vigorously with a wooden spoon.

5 Beat until the mixture is smooth and pulls away from the side of the saucepan to form a ball of dough, about 20 seconds. Return the saucepan to the stove and beat over very low heat to dry out the ball of dough, about 30 seconds. Remove from heat.

Warmth of butter and water mixture cooks flour into ball of dough

6 Beat in 3 of the eggs, one at a time, beating thoroughly after each addition.

Beat in eggs one at a time so dough can absorb egg gradually

When enough egg has been added, dough will become shiny

7 Beat the remaining egg in a small bowl and add it little by little until the dough is shiny and soft.

ANNE SAYS
'You may not need all of the last egg.'

If you fold bag over your hand, it will be easier to fill

8 Fit the piping bag with the nozzle: drop a 1-cm (³/₈-inch) nozzle into the bag. Twist the bag, tucking the bag into the nozzle with your finger.

ANNE SAYS
'Twisting the bag and pushing it down into the nozzle keeps the mixture from leaking during filling.'

9 Fold the top of the piping bag over your hand to form a collar and add the choux dough, scraping a spatula against the folded edge of the bag. When full, tug the bag to straighten it, and twist the top until there is no air left in the bag.

10 Hold the twisted top of the bag between your thumb and forefinger and squeeze the bag gently to press out the dough in 30-35 2.5-cm (1-inch) mounds spaced apart.

2 MAKE THE GLAZE; BAKE THE PUFFS

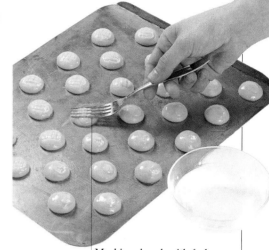

Marking dough with fork
helps it to rise evenly

1 Prepare the egg glaze: beat the egg with the salt so they are well mixed. Leave 2-3 minutes until smooth and the salt softens the egg white.

2 Brush some egg glaze on each choux pastry puff.

! TAKE CARE !
Do not let any glaze fall on the baking sheet; it makes the dough stick and prevents it from rising evenly.

3 Press down lightly on each round with the tines of the fork, first in one direction and then in the other, to make a criss-cross pattern.

4 Bake the choux pastry puffs in the heated oven until the puffs are firm and brown, about 25-30 minutes. Transfer the choux puffs to the wire rack.

Folded tea towel
is good stand-in
for oven gloves

Each puff should be
pleasantly rounded
and golden brown

Egg glaze gives
glossy finish

5 With the small, sharp knife, make a horizontal slit in each puff to release steam. Allow puffs to cool. Meanwhile, if using ice cream made well ahead, allow it to soften in the refrigerator.

3 MAKE THE CHOCOLATE SAUCE AND FINISH THE PROFITEROLES

Stir constantly while heating chocolate and cream to prevent lumping

1 Chop the chocolate and put in a medium heavy-based saucepan with the cream. Heat gently, stirring with a wooden spoon, until the chocolate has melted and the mixture is smooth and thick.

2 If using Cognac, add it to the chocolate-and-cream mixture, and stir until evenly blended. Keep the sauce warm until ready to pour over the profiteroles.

Chocolate ice cream peeps out of airy pastry puffs

Gently separate 2 halves of each profiterole to make room for ice cream

3 Fill each profiterole with a ball of ice cream. Pile the profiteroles in a shallow dish.

¶❶¶ TO SERVE

Pour the warm chocolate sauce over the profiteroles. Serve immediately.

Chocolate sauce is poured over filled profiteroles

94

VARIATION

CHOCOLATE ICE CREAM SWANS

Swans of choux pastry float on a lake of chocolate sauce in this elegant reworking of the profiterole theme.

1 Make the choux pastry as directed in the profiteroles recipe.

2 For 8-12 swan bodies, use a 1.5-mm (³⁄₈-inch) plain nozzle in the piping bag to pipe out ovals, about 4 x 7.5 cm (1½ x 3 inches), on to a buttered baking sheet. Slightly elongate the ovals to form tails. Leave plenty of room for them to double in size while baking.

3 Hold a 5-mm (¼-inch) plain nozzle firmly over the first nozzle already in the piping bag and pipe out 16 S-shaped necks and heads, 7.5-10 cm (3-4 inches) long, on a second buttered baking sheet (this number includes extra to allow for breakages).

4 Brush bodies and necks with egg glaze and bake as directed, allowing 10-15 minutes for the necks and 30-35 minutes for the bodies.

5 Transfer the baked bodies and necks to a wire rack. Cut the oval bodies in half horizontally with the serrated knife, then cut each top piece lengthwise in half for the wings. Allow to cool completely. Transfer the chocolate ice cream to the refrigerator to soften.

6 Make the chocolate sauce as directed in the profiteroles recipe.

7 Fill the bodies with balls of ice cream and insert a neck at the broad end. Arrange the wings in the ice cream at an angle so they spread up and out from the neck. Spoon pools of chocolate sauce on to individual plates. Sift 30-45 ml (2-3 tbsp) icing sugar over the swans and place them on the plates. Serve immediately.

VARIATION

CHOUX CHANTILLY RING

Chocolate-speckled Chantilly cream fills this choux pastry ring.

1 Make the choux pastry as directed.

2 Using a 1.5-mm (⁵⁄₈-inch) nozzle, pipe out a 20-cm (8-inch) diameter ring on to a buttered baking sheet.

3 Pipe a second ring just inside the first. Pipe a third ring on top. Alternatively, spoon out the dough.

4 Brush with egg glaze and bake until firm and brown, 20-30 minutes. Transfer to a wire rack, split the ring horizontally to release the steam, and allow to cool completely.

5 Omit the chocolate ice cream. Make Chantilly cream: whip 500 ml (16 fl oz) double cream in a chilled bowl until soft peaks form. Add 30 ml (2 tbsp) sugar and 5 ml (1 tsp) vanilla essence and whip until stiff peaks form. Stir in 60 g (2 oz) grated chocolate.

6 Spoon or pipe the chocolate-speckled cream on to the bottom of the cooled ring. Set the upper half on top.

7 Make the chocolate sauce as directed, allow to cool slightly, and drizzle a little over the ring using a paper piping cone or a teaspoon. Fill the centre of the ring with whole fresh strawberries. Serve with remaining chocolate sauce handed separately.

BLACK AND WHITE CHOCOLATE MOUSSE TOWERS

🍽 SERVES 8　🥄 WORK TIME 45-50 MINUTES　❄ CHILLING TIME 30 MINUTES

EQUIPMENT

sieve

6-cm (2½-inch) pastry cutter

food processor*

whisk

ladle

chopping board

saucepans

baking parchment

chef's knife

rubber spatula

bowls

piping bag and large star nozzle

palette knife

* blender can also be used

With a touch of art deco elegance, white chocolate mousse is layered with discs of dark chocolate, set on a brilliant background of raspberry coulis, and studded with fresh blueberries. To offset the sweetness of the mousse, fresh blueberries are hidden within the sandwich – substitute raspberries if blueberries are not available. This dessert is such a crowd pleaser, that I've developed two delicious variations on the theme.

GETTING AHEAD

The chocolate discs can be layered with baking parchment and stored in the refrigerator up to 1 week. You can prepare the mousse, assemble the towers and make the raspberry coulis 1 day ahead. Refrigerate them, and arrange on plates just before serving.

metric	SHOPPING LIST	imperial
250 g	plain chocolate	8 oz
375 g	white chocolate	12 oz
375 ml	double cream	12 fl oz
300 g	blueberries	10 oz
For the raspberry coulis		
500 g	raspberries	1 lb
15-30 ml	kirsch (optional)	1-2 tbsp
30-45 ml	icing sugar	2-3 tbsp

INGREDIENTS

white chocolate　plain chocolate

icing sugar

blueberries　raspberries

double cream　kirsch

ANNE SAYS
'Drained, thawed frozen raspberries can be used for the coulis, but they lack the perfume of fresh berries.'

ORDER OF WORK

1 MAKE THE CHOCOLATE DISCS

2 MAKE THE WHITE CHOCOLATE MOUSSE

3 ASSEMBLE THE TOWERS

4 FINISH THE DISH

1 MAKE THE CHOCOLATE DISCS

1 Cut the plain chocolate into large chunks. Chop them with the chef's knife, or in a food processor using the pulse button. Melt the chocolate in a large bowl placed in a saucepan half-filled with hot water.

2 Cut 5 strips of baking parchment, each 36 cm (15 inches) long and 7.5 cm (3 inches) wide. Quickly spread the chocolate on the paper strips to an even layer about 3 mm (1/8 inch) thick. Cool until on the point of setting.

ANNE SAYS
'It's a good idea to make extra strips of chocolate as the discs break easily.'

Spread melted chocolate evenly with palette knife

3 Using the pastry cutter, stamp out at least 24 discs. Leave to set.

ANNE SAYS
'You can also use a glass to cut the discs.'

! TAKE CARE !
Do not refrigerate the discs before they set or the chocolate will shrink away from the paper and buckle.

4 When the chocolate is firm, turn the paper over and carefully peel the paper away from the discs, handling the shapes as little as possible so the chocolate does not melt and become dull. If the discs do not come off easily, re-cut them with the pastry cutter.

Use one hand to pull paper and other as guide

2 MAKE THE WHITE CHOCOLATE MOUSSE

Protect your hands with cloth or oven gloves

Place bowl on damp tea towel to hold it steady as you whisk

1 Chop the white chocolate and put it in a bowl. Bring half of the cream to the boil in a small saucepan and pour it over the chopped chocolate, whisking constantly until the chocolate has melted and is smooth. Allow the mixture to cool completely.

2 Whip the remaining cream until soft peaks form. Fold the whipped cream into the white chocolate mixture. Chill in the refrigerator until firm enough to pipe, about 30 minutes.

3 ASSEMBLE THE TOWERS

1 Make a berry coulis (see box, page 99) with the raspberries. Cover the coulis and chill in the refrigerator. Pick over the blueberries to remove all stems and any blemished fruit.

2 Fill the piping bag and star nozzle with the white chocolate mousse.

3 Pipe out a circle of small mousse rosettes on to a chocolate disc.

ANNE SAYS
'You can spoon on the mousse instead of piping it.'

Gently squeeze bag with one hand and use other as guide

4 With your fingers, arrange a few blueberries in the centre of the rosettes.

Use very light pressure only

5 Set a chocolate disc on top and press it down gently with the end of the palette knife.

6 Add another circle of mousse rosettes and fill with more blueberries.

Press chocolate with palette knife rather than hands to prevent damage to discs

7 Cover with a third chocolate disc and decorate with a large central rosette of mousse. Top the rosette with a blueberry. Repeat with more discs, mousse and blueberries to make a total of 8 towers.

HOW TO MAKE A BERRY COULIS

A coulis is a sauce of a thickish consistency, which can be sweet or savoury, that is most usually made from fruit or vegetables. The word comes from couloir, *a type of antique French sieve. Fleshy fruits, such as berries, produce some of the best coulis. The sauce is the right thickness when it densely coats the back of a spoon.*

1 Pick over raspberries, or hull strawberries or other berries, washing them only if they are dirty. Put the berries in a food processor.

3 Add kirsch, if using, then add icing sugar to taste. Purée again until the sugar is evenly blended with the berries.

2 Work the berries in the machine until they are puréed.

Only fine sieve will catch raspberry seeds

Use ladle to assist sauce through sieve.

4 For raspberries, work the puréed fruit through a fine sieve to remove the seeds.

FINISH THE DISH

1 Ladle a little raspberry coulis on to individual plates.

Use small ladle to help control amount of coulis

Plates with well in centre allow coulis to 'pool' in middle and give neat finishing edge

2 Tip the plates slightly; the sauce will spread evenly over the well in the centre.

3 With the palette knife, carefully transfer the towers to the plates.

Try to place tower exactly in centre of plate

Gently slide tower off palette knife with your fingertips

Use palette knife so chocolate remains cool and is unaffected by heat of your hand

¡©¡ TO SERVE
Arrange the remaining blueberries in a ring round each chocolate mousse tower.

Whole blueberries are placed at regular intervals round chocolate tower to create pretty 'frame'

White chocolate mousse looks dainty piped in tiny rosettes on chocolate discs

Raspberry coulis has been sieved to give smooth, glossy finish

VARIATION

DARK CHOCOLATE WHISKY MOUSSE TOWERS

When a mousse of dark chocolate replaces the white in Black and White Chocolate Mousse Towers, the flavour is even more intense.

1 Chop 250 g (8 oz) plain chocolate, then melt in a saucepan with 60 ml (4 tbsp) water. Remove from the heat and stir in 15 ml (1 tbsp) unsalted butter.
2 Whisk 3 egg yolks into the chocolate mixture, one by one. Whisk the mixture over low heat, about 4 minutes to ensure yolks are cooked. Remove from the heat and whisk in 30 ml (2 tbsp) whisky. Cool until tepid.
3 Dissolve 50 g (1¾ oz) sugar in 60 ml (4 tbsp) water, then boil without stirring to 120°C (248°F) on a sugar thermometer (the hard-ball stage). Whisk 3 egg whites until stiff and gradually whisk in the hot sugar syrup. Continue whisking until the meringue is cool and stiff, 5 minutes. Fold into cool chocolate mixture.
4 Make the dark chocolate discs as directed.
5 Substitute the dark chocolate mousse for the white chocolate mousse and assemble the towers as directed, spooning on the mousse rather than piping it.
6 Serve the towers on a pool of single cream surrounded by blueberries.

VARIATION

MARBLED BLACK AND WHITE CHOCOLATE MOUSSE TOWERS

Contrasting feathers of white in the dark chocolate squares give these mousse towers an art nouveau rather than an art deco look.

1 Chop 30 g (1 oz) white chocolate and melt it as directed.
2 Make a paper piping cone (see box, page 34). Fill it with the melted white chocolate, fold the top to seal and trim the tip.
3 Melt the dark chocolate. With a palette knife, spread it evenly on each of four 6 x 36-cm (2½ x 15-inch) strips of baking parchment. Make feathered chocolate squares (see box, right).
4 Chill the squares until firm, then lift the squares from the paper with the palette knife. Make the mousse.
5 Assemble the towers as directed, using raspberries instead of blueberries, and serve on the raspberry coulis.

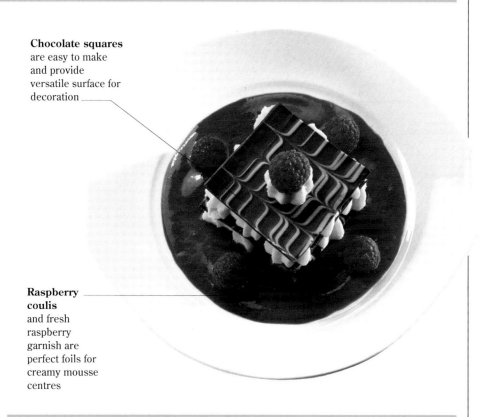

Chocolate squares are easy to make and provide versatile surface for decoration

Raspberry coulis and fresh raspberry garnish are perfect foils for creamy mousse centres

Place whole raspberry in centre of mousse rosettes

HOW TO MAKE FEATHERED CHOCOLATE SQUARES

1 Pipe even lengthwise lines of melted white chocolate over one strip of dark chocolate, about 6 mm (¼ inch) apart.

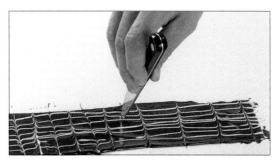

2 Draw the tip of a small knife crosswise through the white chocolate, first in one direction, then in the other, to create feathers. Repeat with the remaining chocolate strips. Leave to stand until almost set, 25-30 minutes.

3 With a large knife, trim the edges of the chocolate strips if necessary and cut them across at 6-cm (2½-inch) intervals, making a total of 24 squares.

CHOCOLATE MOCHA SORBET

 MAKES 1 LITRE (1²/₃ PINTS) TO SERVE 6-8 WORK TIME 25-30 MINUTES* FREEZING TIME AT LEAST 4 HOURS

EQUIPMENT

ice-cream maker

rubber spatula

bowls

kitchen scissors

chef's knife

baking parchment

palette knife

saucepans

metal spoons

wooden spoon

pencil

chopping board

tape

white paper

INGREDIENTS

bittersweet and plain chocolate

instant coffee powder

caster sugar

ANNE SAYS
'*Mocha is a term used to describe many coffee-and-chocolate-flavoured dishes. Coffee's role as a flavour is small but important, and coffee can actually take the place of chocolate in many desserts. For flavouring, a dark roast is best. Instant coffee is the easiest form for adding coffee flavouring because it dissolves. You can also infuse a liquid such as milk with ground coffee beans, heat and leave to stand, then strain.*'

I think you'll like the surprisingly creamy texture of this sorbet, in which coffee combines with chocolate for the popular taste of mocha. Shaped into ovals (or quenelles as they are called in France), the sorbet looks particularly attractive served on individual plates. Home-made chocolate fans add an elegant finishing touch. If you are short of time, you can leave the sorbet plain, or use chocolate coffee beans as a complementary decoration instead.

GETTING AHEAD
The sorbet can be stored in the freezer up to 1 week, but the texture may coarsen. The chocolate fans for the decoration can be layered with baking parchment and stored in the refrigerator up to 1 week.

* plus time to make chocolate fans

ORDER OF WORK

1 MAKE THE SORBET AND FANS

2 SHAPE THE SORBET FOR SERVING

metric	SHOPPING LIST	imperial
90 g	bittersweet chocolate	3 oz
750 ml	water	1 ¼ pints
30-45 ml	instant coffee powder	2-3 tbsp
300 g	caster sugar	10 oz
90 g	plain chocolate for chocolate fans	3 oz

1 MAKE THE SORBET AND FANS

Stirring with wooden spoon ensures sugar is evenly distributed and mixture does not stick

1 Cut the bittersweet chocolate into large chunks. Chop them with the chef's knife, or in a food processor using the pulse button. Put half of the water in a medium heavy-based saucepan, add the chopped chocolate and the coffee and heat, stirring, until melted and smooth.

2 Add the sugar and the remaining water and heat, stirring, until the sugar has dissolved.

3 Bring to the boil and simmer 8-10 minutes, stirring – the mixture should thicken very slightly. Remove from the heat and allow to cool completely.

4 Pour the sorbet mixture into the ice-cream maker and freeze until slushy, following the manufacturer's instructions. Meanwhile, chill a large bowl in the freezer.

Make sure sorbet mixture is completely cold before pouring into ice-cream maker

5 Transfer the sorbet to the chilled bowl, cover it and freeze at least 4 hours to allow the flavour to mellow. Meanwhile, make 12-16 chocolate fans (see box, page 104).

ANNE SAYS
'Freezing time varies greatly with the machine you use.'

HOW TO MAKE PIPED CHOCOLATE SHAPES

Melted chocolate can be piped into initials, fans or baroque curlicues that, when set, can be removed from the paper and used to decorate ices and other desserts.

1 Draw or trace the desired shapes on a sheet of white paper. Tape a sheet of semi-transparent baking parchment to the work surface so it holds, then slide the drawing under the paper.

Press hard with pencil so drawing will show through when under parchment

2 Make a paper piping cone (see box, page 34). Cut the plain chocolate into large chunks. Chop them with a chef's knife, or in a food processor using the pulse button. Melt in a bowl placed in a saucepan half-filled with hot water. Fill the cone with the melted chocolate.

Use light pressure to pipe chocolate

3 Fold over the top of the paper piping cone to seal, and then trim the tip with scissors.

Make several spares as shapes may break

4 Pipe melted chocolate on to the paper following the outline of the drawings and letting the chocolate fall evenly from the tip without forcing it. Leave the chocolate shapes to set at room temperature. When firm, remove carefully with a palette knife, handling them as little as possible so the chocolate does not melt or crack.

! TAKE CARE !
Do not refrigerate the shapes before they are set, because the chocolate will shrink away from the paper and buckle.

2 SHAPE THE SORBET FOR SERVING

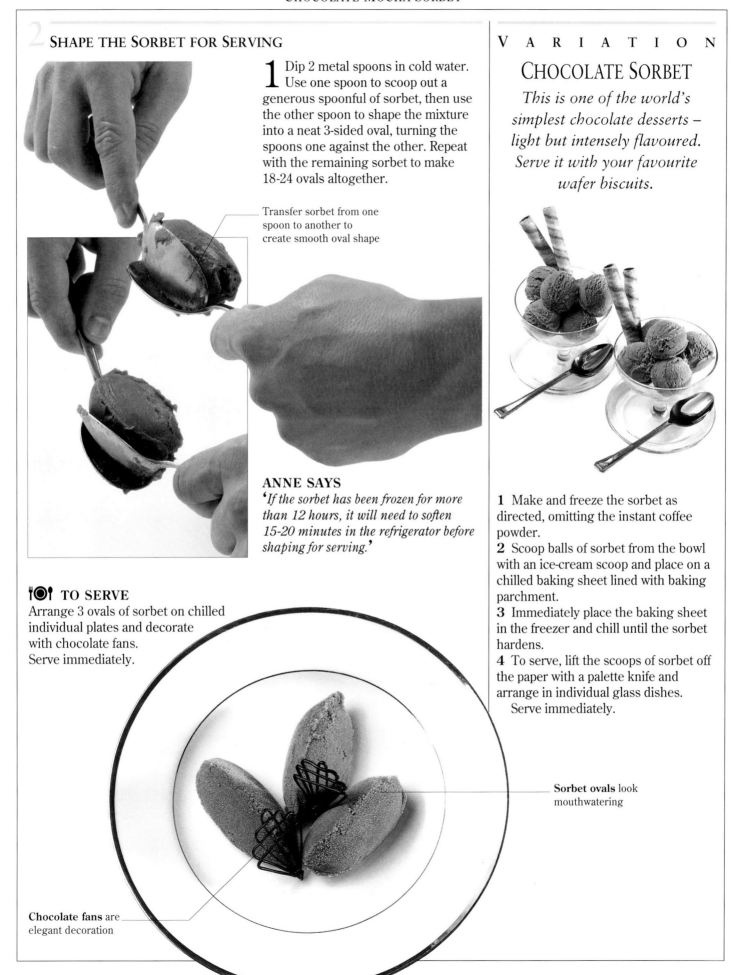

1 Dip 2 metal spoons in cold water. Use one spoon to scoop out a generous spoonful of sorbet, then use the other spoon to shape the mixture into a neat 3-sided oval, turning the spoons one against the other. Repeat with the remaining sorbet to make 18-24 ovals altogether.

Transfer sorbet from one spoon to another to create smooth oval shape

ANNE SAYS
'*If the sorbet has been frozen for more than 12 hours, it will need to soften 15-20 minutes in the refrigerator before shaping for serving.*'

¶❷ TO SERVE
Arrange 3 ovals of sorbet on chilled individual plates and decorate with chocolate fans. Serve immediately.

Chocolate fans are elegant decoration

Sorbet ovals look mouthwatering

VARIATION

CHOCOLATE SORBET
This is one of the world's simplest chocolate desserts – light but intensely flavoured. Serve it with your favourite wafer biscuits.

1 Make and freeze the sorbet as directed, omitting the instant coffee powder.
2 Scoop balls of sorbet from the bowl with an ice-cream scoop and place on a chilled baking sheet lined with baking parchment.
3 Immediately place the baking sheet in the freezer and chill until the sorbet hardens.
4 To serve, lift the scoops of sorbet off the paper with a palette knife and arrange in individual glass dishes.
   Serve immediately.

CHOCOLATE ICE CREAM

 MAKES 1 LITRE (1²/₃ PINTS) TO SERVE 6-8   WORK TIME 15-20 MINUTES   ❄ FREEZING TIME 4-6 HOURS

EQUIPMENT

chef's knife

vegetable peeler

rubber spatula

wooden spoon

bowls   sieve

tea towel

heavy-based medium saucepan

whisk   ice-cream maker

chopping board

baking parchment

ice-cream scoop

Home-made ice cream still beats them all, and chocolate is without doubt the number-one favourite flavour. Here, chocolate curls add a decorative touch. I leave you to choose your own accompaniment – langues de chats or other biscuits, or a colourful assortment of sliced fresh fruit in season such as pineapple, strawberries, peaches and bananas.

GETTING AHEAD

The ice cream can be made up to 2 weeks ahead and kept in a covered container in the freezer. It will be very hard, so let it soften in the refrigerator 30-60 minutes before serving.

INGREDIENTS

plain chocolate

caster sugar

egg yolks   double cream

cornflour

milk

bar plain chocolate

ANNE SAYS
'You will not use the entire bar of chocolate to make the curls for the decoration, but you will need a good-sized bar to be able to make them.'

ORDER OF WORK

1   **MAKE THE CHOCOLATE CUSTARD SAUCE**

2   **FREEZE THE ICE CREAM**

metric	SHOPPING LIST	imperial
250 g	plain chocolate	8 oz
600 ml	milk	1 pint
125 g	caster sugar	4 oz
8	egg yolks	8
30 ml	cornflour	2 tbsp
250 ml	double cream	8 fl oz
1	bar plain chocolate for chocolate curls	1

MAKE THE CHOCOLATE CUSTARD SAUCE

1 With the chef's knife, cut the plain chocolate into large chunks. Chop them with the chef's knife, or in a food processor using the pulse button.

2 Put the milk in the saucepan, add the chopped chocolate and heat, stirring, until melted and smooth.

Add chocolate to milk all at once

Large chef's knife makes for easy chopping

Chocolate is chopped so it will melt easily in milk

3 Add the sugar to the chocolate milk and stir until it has dissolved.

Whisk slowly so bubbles do not form

4 In a medium bowl, whisk the egg yolks with the cornflour.

5 Gradually whisk three-quarters of the chocolate milk into the egg yolk mixture until smooth. Reserve the remainder in a measuring jug.

! TAKE CARE !
Do not overwhisk or the custard will be frothy instead of smooth.

Steady bowl on work surface with folded tea towel as you whisk

Pour custard through sieve to remove any bits of cooked egg yolk

6 Return the mixture to the saucepan and cook over moderate heat, stirring constantly with the wooden spoon, until the custard just comes to the boil and thickens enough to coat the back of the spoon. Allow to cool 1-2 seconds, then lift the spoon out of the custard and run your finger across the spoon: it should leave a clear trail.

! TAKE CARE !
Do not continue to boil the custard once it has thickened or it may curdle.

7 Stir the reserved chocolate milk into the chocolate custard. Strain the chocolate custard sauce into a cold bowl and leave to cool. If the custard sauce forms a skin, whisk to dissolve it.

2 FREEZE THE ICE CREAM

1 Pour the chocolate custard sauce into the ice-cream maker and freeze until slushy, according to the manufacturer's instructions. Meanwhile, chill 2 large bowls in the freezer.

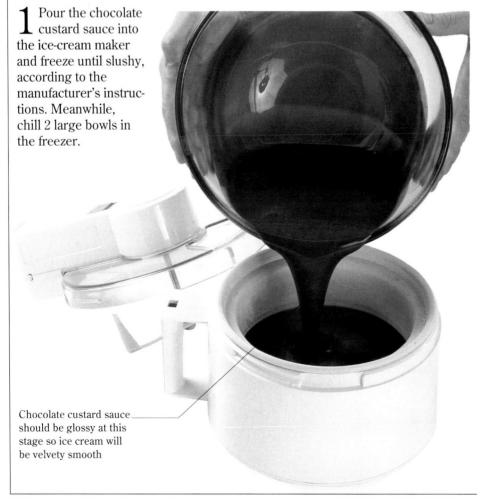

Chocolate custard sauce should be glossy at this stage so ice cream will be velvety smooth

2 Pour the cream into 1 chilled bowl and whip until it forms peaks and holds its shape.

3 Add the whipped cream to the partially-set chocolate custard and continue freezing until firm.

ANNE SAYS
'You'll find that the freezing time for the ice cream varies very much with the machine you use.'

4 Transfer the ice cream to the second chilled bowl, cover and freeze at least 4 hours.

🍽 TO SERVE

Make the chocolate curls: with the vegetable peeler, shave curls from the edge of the chocolate bar on to the baking parchment. Use the ice-cream scoop to form the ice cream into balls and divide among dessert bowls. Sprinkle chocolate curls on top.

Chocolate curls are sprinkled over scoops of ice cream

VARIATION
CHOCOLATE INDULGENCE ICE CREAM

An indulgence indeed, with two kinds of chopped chocolate added to Chocolate Ice Cream.

1 Coarsely chop 125 g (4 oz) plain chocolate and 125 g (4 oz) white chocolate. Alternatively, you can use equal portions of plain chocolate chips and white chocolate chips.
2 Make the chocolate ice cream as directed, adding the chopped chocolates with the whipped cream.
3 Serve scoops of ice cream, decorated with soft fruits, such as raspberries, and fresh mint sprigs.

Langues de chats add crisp contrast to velvety smooth ice cream

VARIATION
CHOCOLATE PRALINE ICE CREAM

When praline is added to Chocolate Ice Cream, the result is crunchy and sweet with a slight tang, the best of all worlds.

1 Make the praline: lightly oil a marble slab or baking sheet. Heat 150 g (5 oz) whole unblanched almonds and 150 g (5 oz) caster sugar in a heavy-based pan until the sugar melts, stirring with a wooden spoon. Continue cooking over fairly low heat to a medium caramel, stirring lightly. The sugar should be a deep golden brown and the almonds should make a popping sound.
2 Immediately pour the mixture on to the slab or baking sheet, spread out with the wooden spoon and leave until cool and crisp, 10-15 minutes.

3 Put the praline into a plastic bag and crack into pieces with a rolling pin, then coarsely grind in a food processor or blender.
4 Make the chocolate ice cream as directed. Reserve some praline for garnish and add the remainder to the ice cream with the whipped cream. Serve scooped into balls, with the reserved praline sprinkled on top.

CHEF FERRE'S FROZEN TRI-CHOCOLATE TERRINE

🍽 MAKES 12-16 SLICES　🥄 WORK TIME 35-40 MINUTES　❄ FREEZING TIME 6-12 HOURS

EQUIPMENT

large terrine
(30 x 7.5 x 7.5 cm/
12 x 3 x 3 inches)

kitchen scissors

chef's knife

pastry brush

bowls

whisk*

wooden spoon

baking parchment

sieve

rubber spatula

wooden rolling pin
without handles

saucepans

roasting tin

chopping board

*electric mixer can also be used

Maurice Ferré has been the pastry chef at Maxim's in Paris for more than 35 years. His frozen chocolate terrine, composed of three sumptuously-flavoured chocolate layers, and sliced to serve with a pool of delicate mint custard sauce, is world famous.

INGREDIENTS

eggs

double cream

egg whites

plain chocolate

white chocolate

milk chocolate

caster sugar

milk

egg yolks

unsalted butter

cornflour

fresh mint

metric	SHOPPING LIST	imperial
	vegetable oil for tin	
	For the chocolate layers	
125 g	plain chocolate	4 oz
135 ml	double cream	9 tbsp
6	eggs	6
135 g	unsalted butter	4 ½ oz
6	egg whites	6
45 ml	caster sugar	3 tbsp
150 g	white chocolate	5 oz
150 g	milk chocolate	5 oz
	For the mint custard sauce	
1	bunch of fresh mint	1
500 ml	milk	16 fl oz
60 g	caster sugar	2 oz
6	egg yolks	6
22.5 ml	cornflour	1 ½ tbsp

ORDER OF WORK

1 MAKE THE DARK CHOCOLATE LAYER

2 MAKE THE WHITE AND MILK CHOCOLATE LAYERS

3 MAKE THE MINT CUSTARD SAUCE

4 TURN OUT THE TERRINE

1 MAKE THE DARK CHOCOLATE LAYER

1 Lightly brush the sides and bottom of the terrine with oil.

ANNE SAYS
'If you like, you can rub the oil on to the tin with kitchen paper.'

2 Using the base of the terrine as a guide, draw and then cut out 2 strips of baking parchment. Use one to line the bottom of the terrine and reserve the other.

3 Cut the plain chocolate into large chunks. Chop them with the chef's knife, or in a food processor using the pulse button. Melt the chocolate in a large bowl placed in a saucepan half-filled with hot water.

4 In a small saucepan, bring 45 ml (3 tbsp) of the double cream just to boiling point, then whisk it into the melted chocolate.

Whisk constantly while adding cream so it mixes smoothly into chocolate

Mix in each batch of butter completely before adding more

5 Separate 2 of the eggs. Whisk the egg yolks into the chocolate mixture one by one, stirring well before adding the second yolk.

6 Cut 45 g (1 ½ oz) of the butter into small pieces and add, a few pieces at a time, whisking so the butter melts smoothly into the warm mixture.

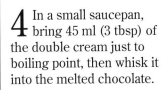

7 In another large bowl, whisk 4 of the egg whites until stiff.

ANNE SAYS
'*If using an electric mixer, beat the whites on medium speed until they become foamy and white, then increase the speed to maximum.*'

Whisk whites until stiff peaks form

8 Sprinkle in 15 ml (1 tbsp) of the sugar and whisk until glossy, about 20 seconds, to make a light meringue.

Dark chocolate mixture forms top layer when terrine is turned out

9 Fold the meringue into the chocolate mixture as lightly as possible. This can be done in 2 batches, if you like.

10 Pour the dark chocolate mixture into the terrine.

! TAKE CARE !
Made this way, the terrine contains uncooked eggs. You can, if you like, cook the chocolate mixture over low heat about 4 minutes, whisking constantly, to ensure that the eggs are thoroughly cooked, with no danger of salmonella contamination. However, the terrine will be less fluffy and light.

Scrape inside of bowl to remove all mixture

11 Spread the chocolate mixture in the terrine, pushing it into the corners and smoothing the top evenly. Freeze 30-40 minutes while preparing the remaining layers.

2 MAKE THE WHITE AND MILK CHOCOLATE LAYERS

1 Follow the instructions for making the dark chocolate layer, using white instead of plain chocolate. Pour the white chocolate mixture into the terrine.

2 Spread over the dark chocolate layer and freeze, 30-40 minutes.

Be sure dark chocolate layer is firmly set before pouring on white chocolate mixture

3 Make the milk chocolate layer, using the same process as for the preceding layers, and pour it into the terrine on top of the white chocolate layer.

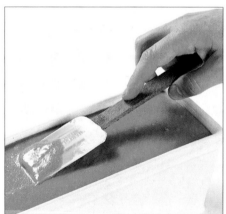

4 Smooth the top layer using the rubber spatula.

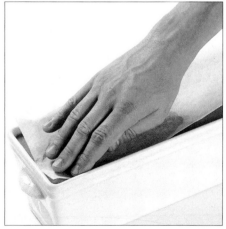

Milk chocolate mixture should almost reach top of terrine

5 Lightly press the reserved piece of baking parchment on top of the milk chocolate layer. Chill the terrine in the freezer until firm, at least 6 hours.

3 MAKE THE MINT CUSTARD SAUCE

1 Rinse the mint and trim the ends of the stalks. Reserve 12-16 sprigs for decoration and lightly crush the remainder using the rolling pin.

Press down and rotate end of pin to bruise and soften mint leaves

Make sure prettiest sprigs are set aside for decoration

Reserve pan as sauce will be returned to it but wipe out any remaining mint

2 Put the milk in a heavy-based saucepan and bring just to the boil. Add the crushed mint, cover and leave to infuse in a warm place 10-15 minutes.

3 Strain the milk into a measuring jug or bowl and discard the crushed mint. Stir in the sugar until dissolved.

Use conical sieve to direct liquid into measure

4 Whisk the egg yolks with the cornflour in a medium bowl. Add the infused milk, reserving about 125 ml (4 fl oz). Whisk until just smooth, then return the custard to the saucepan.

Whisk only until custard is smooth or it will be too frothy

5 Cook over moderate heat, stirring constantly with the wooden spoon, until the custard just comes to the boil and thickens enough to coat the back of the spoon. (Your finger will leave a clear trail across the spoon.) Stir in the reserved milk. Strain the custard into a chilled bowl and leave to cool.

4 TURN OUT THE TERRINE

1 Fill the roasting tin with hot water. Dip the base of the terrine into the hot water 10-15 seconds, then lift it out and dry it. Peel the baking parchment off the top.

2 Set a rectangular serving dish on top of the terrine and turn them over together. Remove the terrine.

ANNE SAYS
'If the terrine sticks to the tin, run a knife dipped in hot water round the sides, between the terrine and the mould.'

3 Peel off the paper. Leave the terrine to soften in the refrigerator about 1 hour, then cut it into 2-2.5 cm (³/₄-1 inch) thick slices. Serve with mint custard sauce and mint sprig decoration.

Baking parchment peels away easily from terrine

Mint custard sauce should be served on the side

VARIATION

TRI-CHOCOLATE TERRINE ON STRAWBERRY COULIS

The vibrant colour and taste of strawberry provide natural foils for the rich chocolate in Chef Ferré's Tri-Chocolate Terrine.

1 Make the terrine as directed and freeze.

2 Omit the mint custard sauce and instead prepare a strawberry coulis: hull 650 g (1¼ lb) strawberries, washing them only if they are dirty, then purée them in a food processor or blender. Add 30 ml (2 tbsp) kirsch, if desired, and 30-45 ml (2-3 tbsp) icing sugar, then purée again.

3 Slice the terrine, then place the slices on individual plates. Cut each slice diagonally in half, and separate the halves slightly. Spoon strawberry coulis in between, and decorate with halved strawberries.

Mint sprig is perfect decoration

— **GETTING AHEAD** —
The terrine can be made up to 2 weeks ahead and frozen. The mint custard sauce can be made 1 day ahead and stored in the refrigerator.

CHOCOLATE AND APRICOT BOMBE

EQUIPMENT

ice-cream maker

rubber spatula

bowls　　　　sieve

saucepans

whisk**　　bombe mould***

wooden spoon

sugar thermometer (optional)

palette knife

chef's knife　　chopping board

piping bag and medium star nozzle

baking parchment

**electric mixer can also be used
***deep metal bowl can be used

A bombe was once spherical, hence its name. Now it usually has a flat base and is moulded in layers with a rich, creamy centre. The apricot filling, flavoured with complementary kirsch, is so good that no one will notice if, to save time, you enclose it in store-bought instead of home-made chocolate ice cream.

* plus time to make ice cream

metric	SHOPPING LIST	imperial
½ quantity	Chocolate Ice Cream (see page 106)	½ quantity
60 g	plain chocolate, for chocolate triangles	2 oz
For the apricot bombe mixture		
125 g	dried apricots	4 oz
4	egg yolks	4
200 g	granulated sugar	6 ½ oz
60 ml	water	4 tbsp
30-45 ml	kirsch	2-3 tbsp
125 ml	double cream	4 fl oz
For the chocolate fudge sauce		
125 g	plain chocolate	4 oz
125 ml	water	4 fl oz
60 g	unsalted butter	2 oz
30 ml	light brown sugar	2 tbsp
	salt	
To finish		
125 ml	double cream	4 fl oz
10 ml	caster sugar	2 tsp
canned apricots for garnish (optional)		

INGREDIENTS

dried apricots

plain chocolate

egg yolks　　light brown sugar

granulated sugar

kirsch

unsalted butter

double cream

chocolate ice cream

canned apricots

ORDER OF WORK

1　LINE THE MOULD AND PREPARE THE APRICOT FILLING

2　MAKE THE CHOCOLATE TRIANGLES

3　MAKE THE CHOCOLATE FUDGE SAUCE

4　TURN OUT AND DECORATE THE BOMBE

1 LINE THE MOULD AND PREPARE THE APRICOT FILLING

Try to spread ice cream in even layer so bombe looks neat when cut

1 Chill the bombe mould in the freezer. With the rubber spatula, spread the ice cream over the bottom and up the side of the mould in a 2.5-5-cm (1-2-inch) layer, leaving a neat, even hollow in the centre. Freeze until firm, 30-60 minutes.

ANNE SAYS
'*To be spreadable, the ice cream must be soft. Home-made ice cream should be used immediately after freezing in the ice-cream maker. If made ahead, let it soften in the refrigerator about 30 minutes.*'

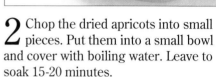

2 Chop the dried apricots into small pieces. Put them into a small bowl and cover with boiling water. Leave to soak 15-20 minutes.

Chill bombe mould so ice cream does not melt

5 Continue whisking at high speed until the mixture is cool, very thick and pale, about 5 minutes.

3 Put the egg yolks in a large bowl and whisk until just mixed.

4 Heat the sugar and water in a small pan until dissolved. Boil until the syrup reaches the soft-ball stage (115°C/239°F) on the thermometer. Gradually pour syrup into egg yolks, whisking constantly.

ANNE SAYS
'*To test the syrup without a thermometer, take the pan from the heat. Dip a teaspoon in the hot syrup and take a little between your finger and thumb – it should form a soft ball.*'

As sugar syrup is whisked into egg yolks, mixture becomes thick and increases in volume

6 Turn the apricots into the sieve and drain off the liquid.

7 Return the apricots to the small bowl. Add the kirsch and mix well with the apricots.

8 Pour the cream into a bowl placed in a larger bowl of iced water. Whip until it just holds its shape.

Rubber spatula is good for mixing ingredients together well

9 Add the apricot mixture to the egg yolk and sugar mixture and stir together.

10 Add the whipped cream to the apricot bombe mixture. Fold the cream into the mixture: cut down into the centre of the bowl, scoop under the contents and turn them over in a rolling motion. At the same time, with your other hand, turn the bowl anti-clockwise.

11 Remove the ice-cream-lined mould from the freezer and pour in the apricot bombe mixture.

ANNE SAYS
'*If the apricots have sunk to the bottom of the cream mixture, stir well before pouring it into the mould.*'

12 Use the palette knife to press the mixture well into the centre of the mould and to smooth the top level. Cover with a piece of baking parchment and the lid and freeze until very firm, 9-12 hours. Meanwhile, make the chocolate triangles.

2 MAKE THE CHOCOLATE TRIANGLES

1 Cut the chocolate into large chunks. Chop them with the chef's knife, or in a food processor using the pulse button. Melt the chocolate in a bowl placed in a saucepan half-filled with hot water and leave to cool. Cut a strip of baking parchment 20 cm (8 inches) long and 2.5 cm (1 inch) wide. Spread the cooled, melted chocolate on the paper to an even layer about 1.5 mm (1/16 inch) thick. Allow to cool until on the point of setting.

2 With the chef's knife, mark the strip of chocolate into triangles without cutting the paper. (Or use a pastry cutter to form discs, crescents, or other shapes of your choice. For a curved shape, lift the strip of paper on to a rolling pin.) Allow to set.

! TAKE CARE !
Do not refrigerate the chocolate shapes before they are set, or they will shrink away from the paper and buckle.

3 When the chocolate is firm, lift the paper away from the work surface, then carefully peel the chocolate away from the paper, using the palette knife to slide between paper and chocolate. Handle the shapes as little as possible so the chocolate does not melt and become dull.

3 MAKE THE CHOCOLATE FUDGE SAUCE

1 Chop the chocolate. Put the water into a heavy-based saucepan. Add the chocolate and heat, stirring, until the chocolate has melted.

2 Dice the butter and add to the saucepan, then add the brown sugar. Bring to the boil, stirring so the ingredients are well mixed.

3 Simmer, stirring occasionally, until thick, 5-7 minutes. Stir in a pinch of salt and keep the sauce warm while you turn out the bombe.

4 TURN OUT AND DECORATE THE BOMBE

1 Whip the cream with the caster sugar until stiff peaks form (see box, page 120). Fill the pastry bag with the whipped cream. Set aside.

Fold top of piping bag over your hand so it forms collar

Warm knife under hot running tap, then wipe dry before running knife round side of mould

3 Remove the lid and baking parchment. Dry the base of the mould and run a knife round the side of the bombe.

When bombe is loosened, ice cream melts a little

2 Remove the mould from the freezer. Dip the mould in a bowl of cool water 30-60 seconds to loosen the bombe from the mould.

4 Set a chilled serving plate on top of the mould and invert them, holding them firmly together.

ANNE SAYS
'If the bombe sticks, hold a hot damp cloth against the mould for several seconds.'

Make sure serving plate is chilled

5 Lift the mould straight up and off the bombe. Wipe the plate to remove any melted ice cream. In hot weather, return the bombe to the freezer.

HOW TO WHIP AND SWEETEN CREAM AND MAKE CHANTILLY CREAM

Double cream, with a minimum 36% butterfat content, is best for whipping, and it should be thoroughly chilled. Chantilly cream is whipped cream flavoured with sugar and vanilla essence, brandy, rum, or a liqueur such as Grand Marnier. Whipped cream can be covered and refrigerated up to 4 hours. It may separate slightly but will thicken again if whipped briefly.

! TAKE CARE !
If the cream is to be piped for decoration, take care not to overwhip it because the cream will be worked further when forced through the piping bag. If too stiff, it will separate.

1 Pour the double cream into a chilled medium-sized bowl placed in a larger bowl of iced water.

2 Whip until the cream forms soft peaks.

3 Add the sugar, and for Chantilly cream, the flavouring, and whip until the cream forms soft peaks again and just holds its shape.

Cream will soften slightly when sugar is added

Whisk will leave clear marks in cream

4 For stiff peaks, continue whipping until the whisk leaves clear marks in the cream.

! TAKE CARE !
If overwhipped, the cream will separate and turn to butter. When this is about to happen, it looks granular.

6 Pipe a ring of sweetened whipped cream rosettes round the base of the bombe.

ANNE SAYS
'For a few moments, the bombe will frost with moisture after turning out, but this will evaporate by the time the bombe is ready to serve.'

Squeeze bag gently with one hand only to push out cream

Use free hand to guide bag

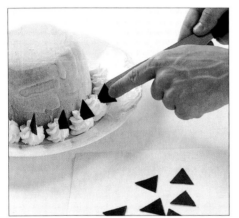

7 When the ring of rosettes is complete, pick up the chocolate triangles, using the palette knife, and tip one into the centre of each rosette. If you like, arrange slices of canned apricots round edge of plate.

Apricot slices add colour and complement filling

Warm fudge sauce is optional

¶◯¶ TO SERVE
Cut the bombe into wedges. Put the wedges on chilled individual plates and serve the warm fudge sauce separately.

BOMBE ROYALE

1 Make full quantity of Chocolate Ice Cream (see page 106).
2 Cut 500 g (1 lb) home-made or bought Swiss roll (preferably filled with apricot jam) into 5 mm (¼ inch) thick slices.
3 Halve the slices and use to line the bottom and side of the mould, fitting them together as tightly as possible so there are no gaps. Chop the leftover pieces and place in a bowl.
4 Mix together 90 ml (6 tbsp) orange juice and 45 ml (3 tbsp) apricot brandy. Brush the Swiss roll lining with this mixture. Mix the remainder with the chopped Swiss roll to moisten. Put the mould in the freezer until firm.
5 Spoon the ice cream into the lined mould and slightly hollow out the centre. Put the chopped Swiss roll in the centre and cover with more ice cream. Freeze until firm.
6 Turn out bombe as directed and pipe whipped cream rosettes on top and round base. Decorate with chocolate fans (see box, page 104) if you like.

— GETTTING AHEAD —
The bombe can be made and stored in the freezer up to 1 week. The chocolate triangles can be layered with baking parchment and stored in the refrigerator up to 1 week. Refrigerate the fudge sauce in a covered container and reheat it in a water bath. Whip the cream, turn out the bombe, and decorate it just before serving.

CHOCOLATE KNOW-HOW

Chocolate is made from the bean of the cacao tree. The beans are made into a thick paste through a process of drying, roasting and grinding. The paste is 'conched', or compressed by rollers, to make it smooth and mellow. The flavour of the chocolate depends on the selection of beans and how they are processed.

TYPES OF CHOCOLATE

The two main components of chocolate are cocoa solids and a light yellow fat called cocoa butter. Different types of block chocolate contain different proportions of the two, together with flavourings and sugar. The finest block chocolate always contains a high proportion of both cocoa solids and cocoa butter, on average they make up 35 per cent of the chocolate, though they can make up as much as 50 per cent or even 70 per cent. In inferior types of chocolate, vegetable oils or shortening may be substituted for cocoa butter.

Because the different types of chocolate give different results during cooking, it is important to use the type specified in the recipe.

PLAIN OR DARK CHOCOLATE

This type of chocolate contains enough sugar to make it good to eat alone. This is the type most commonly used in cooking. The amounts of cocoa solids, cocoa butter, sugar and flavourings vary enormously from brand to brand, so it is well worth experimenting until you find a particular brand that you prefer.

BITTERSWEET CHOCOLATE

This chocolate has a high proportion of cocoa solids and cocoa butter (sometimes as much as 70 per cent), and a small percentage of sugar. It can be hard to find so I use it in recipes only when strictly necessary.

WHITE CHOCOLATE

White chocolate contains cocoa butter (the amount varies according to individual brands) and it has no cocoa solids. Be sure to read the label because inferior brands of white chocolate contain vegetable oil and lack the taste of true chocolate.

MILK CHOCOLATE

In this type of chocolate, dried milk, or sometimes condensed milk, replaces some of the cocoa solids, producing a sweeter taste. Milk chocolate is more sensitive to heat and a bit harder to work with, so it is less commonly used in cooking and garnishing. I've used it in a few of my recipes where I want to create a contrast of taste and colour with plain chocolate.

COCOA POWDER

This is pure unsweetened chocolate from which much of the cocoa butter has been extracted. Dutch-process or alkalised cocoa is the best as its flavour is mild and it dissolves easily. Cocoa is often used for giving cakes and desserts a light dusting of chocolate, particularly where there is a creamy filling or topping, and for adding to basic mixtures.

Sweetened cocoa, also called powdered chocolate, may have powdered milk added to it, and it is often used for drinks. Do not confuse it with the unsweetened cocoa powder I use in my recipes.

COVERING CHOCOLATE

Often called dipping chocolate, coating chocolate or couverture, this has a high cocoa butter content, which makes it very smooth and glossy. It is available in plain, white and milk chocolate varieties. This is chef's chocolate, ideal for dipping because the high cocoa butter content means it melts easily and smoothly, and produces decorations with a high gloss.

STORING CHOCOLATE

Ideally chocolate should be kept cool at around 16°C (60°F) in a dry, airy place. If chocolate is refrigerated, keep it in the vegetable drawer. Seal opened chocolate tightly from humidity and store it away from ingredients with strong odours. In good conditions, dark chocolate can be kept three months or more, longer than the white or milk chocolates that contain a high proportion of milk solids. Chocolate decorations can be stored in the refrigerator or freezer for a week or two, once they are set. If poorly stored, chocolate can develop a whitish film of cocoa butter or sugar. The film looks unattractive, but does not affect flavour; chocolate with this film can still be melted, but it is unsuitable for grating.

WORKING WITH CHOCOLATE

With just a few simple chocolate techniques, you can create a wide variety of fillings, sauces and decorations. All of these techniques are pictured in detail in individual recipes.

CHOPPING AND GRATING CHOCOLATE

When chopping or grating, it is important that the chocolate is firm, so on a warm day refrigerate it first. If you are chopping by hand, touch the chocolate as little as possible and, if you are going to melt the chocolate afterwards, be sure the chopping board is dry, because any moisture can affect the melting consistency of the chocolate.

To chop by hand: with a large chef's knife, chop the chocolate using the broad end, not the tip, of the blade.

To chop in a food processor: cut the chocolate into small chunks and chop it using the pulse button. Do not overwork the chocolate or the heat of the machine can melt it. If necessary, process the chocolate in several batches.

To grate chocolate: hold it firmly with a piece of foil or baking parchment and work it against the coarsest grid of the grater. Let the grated chocolate fall on to a sheet of baking parchment or a plate.

MELTING CHOCOLATE

There are a number of methods for melting chocolate. It is important that the container is uncovered and dry because any water or steam that comes in contact with the chocolate will cause it to seize or harden (see below right).

First, chop the chocolate in chunks of about the same size. A double boiler is good for melting chocolate, or you can place a metal or glass bowl in a pan of water (a water bath). The water should be hot but not simmering. You can also put the chopped chocolate on an ovenproof plate, then melt it over a pan of simmering water.

Once the chocolate starts to melt, stir it occasionally until melted and smooth, then take it from the heat. If the chocolate does seize, stir in white vegetable fat or oil, one teaspoon at a time, until the chocolate is smooth again. Some cooks prefer to melt chocolate in a microwave oven. Medium power is recommended and timing depends on the output of your microwave oven and the type and amount of chocolate. For instance, 60 g (2 oz) of chopped plain chocolate takes about two minutes on Medium power.

TEMPERING CHOCOLATE

Tempering melted chocolate makes it more malleable and shiny for decorations. Covering chocolate (couverture) is the type most often used for tempering because it has a high cocoa butter content and achieves the greatest gloss.

Melt the chocolate in the top of a double boiler or in a bowl placed in a water bath. Heat gently over hot but not simmering water, stirring with a wooden spoon until the chocolate is very smooth and reaches 46°C (115°F) on a sugar thermometer, five to seven minutes. Place the bowl of melted chocolate in a bowl of cool (not iced) water. Stir the chocolate often until it cools to 27°C (80°F), three to five minutes. Then set the chocolate over the pan of hot water again and heat it to 32°C (90°F). It is now ready to use.

PIPING CHOCOLATE

Disposable paper piping cones are useful for piping small amounts of chocolate.

To make two cones, fold a 20 x 35-cm (8 x 14-inch) rectangle of baking parchment in half diagonally and cut along the fold. Fold the short side of one triangle over to the right-angled corner to form a cone shape. Holding the cone together with one hand, wrap the long point of the triangle around the paper cone. Tuck the point of paper inside the cone to secure it. Repeat with the remaining triangle to make another cone.

Fill one cone with melted, cooled chocolate and fold the top to seal. If you need a second one, fill it with chocolate, seal and keep it in a warm place so the chocolate does not set.

If piping directly on a cake or dessert, first snip the tip of the paper cone with scissors. Using light pressure, pipe the design or lettering in an even motion. For instructions on piping separate designs, look at the section on chocolate decorations (see page 124).

! TAKE CARE !

If chocolate is not carefully handled, it will separate or 'seize', suddenly turning into a thick rough mass. This can be corrected by stirring in one or two teaspoons of white vegetable fat or oil until the chocolate becomes smooth again.

*If melted chocolate comes into contact with a small amount of liquid or steam, it will seize.

*If you try to melt chocolate over too small a quantity of liquid, it may seize.

*All other ingredients should be at a similar temperature when mixed with melted chocolate. Adding a hotter liquid can cause the chocolate to seize, while cold liquid can make it lumpy.

*Chocolate will scorch or seize if it is overheated during melting.

CHOCOLATE DECORATIONS

Melted chocolate can be transformed into many different shapes that can be used to decorate cakes and desserts of all kinds. Chocolate can also be piped into scrolls, fans, or lattices, or used for dipping fruit and nuts. Before trying these decorations, be sure to consult the information on working with chocolate on page 123.

MAKING CHOCOLATE LEAVES

Choose pliable leaves with deep veins, such as rose. Using a pastry brush or your fingertip, spread cooled melted chocolate on the shiny side of each leaf in a thin even layer, leaving a little of the stem exposed so the leaf can be peeled off easily. Place the leaves on a plate and allow to cool, then refrigerate until set. With the tips of your fingers, peel each leaf away from the chocolate. Handle the chocolate leaves as little as possible so they do not melt or become dull.

MAKING A CHOCOLATE RIBBON

A chocolate ribbon is a broad strip of chocolate that can be wrapped round an iced cake for an elegant presentation. Cut a strip of baking parchment as wide as the cake is high and long enough to wrap round the cake, allowing a little overlap. (For a glossy ribbon, the chocolate should be tempered.) Brush the paper strip with cooled, melted chocolate, spreading it in an even layer about a 1.5 mm ($^1/_{16}$ inch) thick. Immediately wrap the ribbon round the cake, paper side out. Refrigerate until the chocolate is set, about one hour, then gently peel back the paper.

MAKING CHOCOLATE CURLS

Short curls of chocolate are a quick and easy topping for cakes and desserts. The chocolate should be at room temperature (about 21°C/70°F) so that it is easy to shape. Covering chocolate (couverture), plain, milk or white chocolate can all be used, whichever you prefer. Hold a bar of chocolate at an angle and, with a vegetable peeler, shave away curls of chocolate. Work over a plate or piece of paper, so that the curls can be transferred to the dessert easily, without breaking or melting in your hands.

MAKING CHOCOLATE ROUNDS, SQUARES OR TRIANGLES

Spread melted chocolate evenly with a palette knife in 1.5 mm ($^1/_{16}$ inch) layer over a strip of baking parchment . Leave to cool until on the point of setting. For rounds, whether small coins, or larger discs, use a round pastry cutter or the top of a sharp-edged glass to cut the shapes. For triangles, when on the point of setting, mark the chocolate with a sharp knife without cutting through the paper. Make squares in the same way, cutting the chocolate with a knife when on the point of setting. For all shapes, once the chocolate has been cut, leave it on the paper until fully set, then carefully peel the chocolate away from the paper using a palette knife.

PIPING CHOCOLATE DECORATIONS

Rather than piping designs freehand, you will find it easier to draw or trace them first in pencil on a sheet of paper. Then place a piece of baking parchment on top so the design shows through, and fasten the papers to the work surface with sticky tape.

Cut off the tip of a paper piping cone filled with melted chocolate. Using light pressure, pipe melted chocolate on to the paper, following the outline of your drawing, letting the chocolate fall evenly from the tip without forcing it.

Leave the shapes to set at room temperature. Once set, remove the decorations carefully with a palette knife, handling them as little as possible so the chocolate does not melt or become dull.

CHOCOLATE-DIPPED FRUIT AND NUTS

Fresh, dried, or candied fruits such as sliced banana, cherries, and strawberries dipped in melted chocolate look very pretty arranged round the edge of a cake or dessert, or grouped together in clusters in the centre.

The larger-shaped nut varieties can be hand-dipped in chocolate, too, and used as a decoration.

HOW-TO BOXES

Some basic techniques are general to a number of recipes; they are shown in extra detail in these special 'How-to' boxes:

INDEX

126

ACKNOWLEDGEMENTS

Photographer David Murray
Photographer's Assistant Jules Selmes

Chef Laurent Terrasson
Cookery Consultant Linda Collister
Home Economist Annie Nichols

UK Editor José Northey
Indexer Sally Poole

Typesetting Rowena Feeny
Debbie Rhodes
Text film by Disc To Print (UK) Limited

Production Consultant Lorraine Baird

*Carroll & Brown Limited
would like to thank Chef Eric Treuille for
supplying culinary expertise and Joanna Pitchfork
for her editorial help.
ICTC (081-568-4179) supplied the Cuisinox
Elysee pans used throughout the book.*

*Anne Willan
would like to thank her chief editor
Cynthia Nims and associate editor Kate Krader
for their vital help with writing the book and
researching and testing the recipes, aided by
La Varenne's chefs and trainees.*